THE STORY OF
THE ITALIAN RENAISSANCE

Second Edition

by
Suzanne Strauss Art

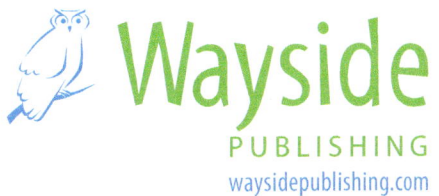

Wayside
PUBLISHING
waysidepublishing.com

For Titania, Letty, and Matilda

Copyright © 2014 by Wayside Publishing

Printed in the USA

1st Printing

Print Date: 117

ISBN 978-1-938026-79-9

CONTENTS

Acknowledgements 4

To The Teacher 5

Prologue 7

Chapter 1: *The Dawning of a New Age* 9

Chapter 2: *Artistic Awakenings* 27

Chapter 3: *The Italian City-States* 39

Chapter 4: *The Age Of The Medici* 57

Chapter 5: *The High Renaissance* 85

Chapter 6: *The Italian Wars* 117

Index 124

ACKNOWLEDGEMENTS

I am very grateful for the aid and encouragement given me by my family - my husband Bob, my son David, and my daughter Robyn. They cheered me on when I first came up with the idea of writing this book and even joined me in Tuscany, where together we analyzed firsthand the art and architecture of the fourteenth and fifteenth centuries. Bob, David, and Robyn contributed their own expertise in the areas of Renaissance history, art, and literature and helped to edit the final manuscript. This book is, in many ways, a family project.

As ever, I am indebted to my students at Fay. Their enthusiastic response to my history units and their wonderful, unbridled curiosity about all manner of things has been a major inspiration for all of the books I have written. And once again, I must thank my friend and colleague, Dick Upjohn of the Fay History Department, for tirelessly reading my manuscript and offering excellent and insightful criticisms.

TO THE TEACHER

The Italian Renaissance was one of history's most fascinating epochs. It was a lavish spectacle of colorful characters, spicy political intrigues, exciting scientific discoveries, and unprecedented achievements in art, architecture, literature, and philosophy. This explosion of creative activity was sparked when medieval scholars delved into the ancient past and liked what they saw. Their efforts to rekindle the intellectual brilliance of earlier times enabled European society to emerge from an age of fear and superstition. Once again the needs and potentials of the individual were valued as much as universal religious beliefs, and the classical balance of reason and faith was restored. The old gloom and doom were replaced by a new spirit of optimism. Man wasn't evil, he was good! And there was plenty to celebrate. During the fruitful years of the fifteenth and sixteenth centuries, an amazing number of talented people became caught up in the flurry and accomplished things that helped usher in the modern age.

Like my other books in the *Early Times* series, this one stresses the story element of history in an effort to "bring alive" the personalities and happenings of the times. I have tried to highlight the principle threads that run through the period and to make frequent connections between the main events and the major players. I have included many challenging words and expressions to pique a student's curiosity and broaden his vocabulary. The content level of the book is appropriate for middle school as well as higher level history courses.

Petrarch was an Italian scholar of the fourteenth century who loved to read books, especially those written in the days of ancient Rome. Petrarch had a vivid imagination and could easily envision the society of those early times. He marveled at the glowing descriptions of the model Roman citizen who made the most of his opportunities and contributed his talents to the local government. Early Rome was a clean city of gleaming marble government buildings, theaters, temples, arenas, and public baths. There was even fresh running water. What a contrast the ancient world posed to medieval Europe, where no one seemed interested in self-improvement, where the government was often mired in political corruption, and where sewers ran down the center of the narrow city streets. And hardly anyone could read or write. Petrarch came to the conclusion that the generations who lived between the fall of the mighty Roman Empire and his own age (a mere one thousand years!) had achieved little of value. Western society seemed to have forgotten the rich heritage of the past and had fallen into a deep slumber. But now it was time to wake up!

Petrarch devoted much of his life to reviving an interest in the culture of ancient Rome. He tirelessly tracked down long forgotten books by Latin authors in the libraries of monasteries and pondered their words. He also wrote his own volumes about the history and personalities of those earlier, richer times, hoping that the qualities of character and mind that made Rome a great power could be applied to improve his own society. His enthusiasm for antiquity was shared by other scholars, and before long it spawned a new interest in the potential of mankind that slowly spread throughout much of Italy, reaching its peak in the sixteenth century. We know this period as the Renaissance.

This extraordinary age glows like a bright star in the history of western literature and art. *Renaissance* is a French word meaning "rebirth." But the movement involved more than the recovery of the ideals of the past. Rather, what began as a revival of ancient values gradually evolved into a spirit of inquisitiveness about all sorts of things. People looked in a new way at the makeup of the natural world and wondered about man's place in it. Theologians consulted ancient texts and used their powers of reason to arrive at conclusions that often conflicted with the long established doctrines of the Church. Suddenly there were multitudes of questions being asked, and the answers led to even more questions. Curiosity had at last been unbridled. One scholar joyfully remarked that he felt like a dwarf standing on the shoulders of a giant. He was raised up by the achievements of antiquity (this was the giant) and yet able to see further than his distant ancestors ever had.

The Renaissance was an exciting time to be alive. Liberated from many of the fears and superstitions of the Middle Ages, imaginative men and women became caught up in the excitement of discovery. Artists, poets, and philosophers were inspired to give form to their own visions of the human condition. Scientists dramatically expanded their horizons of knowledge of the natural world. Learning was a joyful experience, and the air was filled with optimism. Humanist Leon Battista Alberti summed it up the spirit of the age this way: "men can do all things if they will"

But it all started in ancient Italy, so it's there that our story begins.

CHAPTER 1

THE DAWNING OF A NEW AGE

The mighty Romans flexed their muscles and strutted around the ancient world for nearly a thousand years. Fearless generals like Julius Caesar managed to conquer a vast empire that eventually encircled the Mediterranean Sea. During the reign of Augustus, Roman civilization was at its peak. His subjects were governed by an intricate web of officials, guided in everyday matters by a practical system of written laws, and defended by an invincible army.

Roman Arts

Augustus rebuilt the city of Rome; its gleaming marble temples and government buildings symbolized the power and majesty of the emperor. A central feature of Roman architecture was the arch, a graceful structure that can support a tremendous amount of weight. Roman architects designed bridges, aqueducts, and amphitheaters using the arch. They later discovered that by constructing a circle of arches around a central point they could create a large, open space - the dome.

Roman culture was greatly enriched by the conquest of the highly sophisticated civilization of Greece. Manuscripts by Greek authors on all sorts of subjects were translated into Latin, the official language of the Empire. And the Romans became so enamored with the Greek gods of Mount Olympus that they transformed them into Roman deities, changing their names from Greek

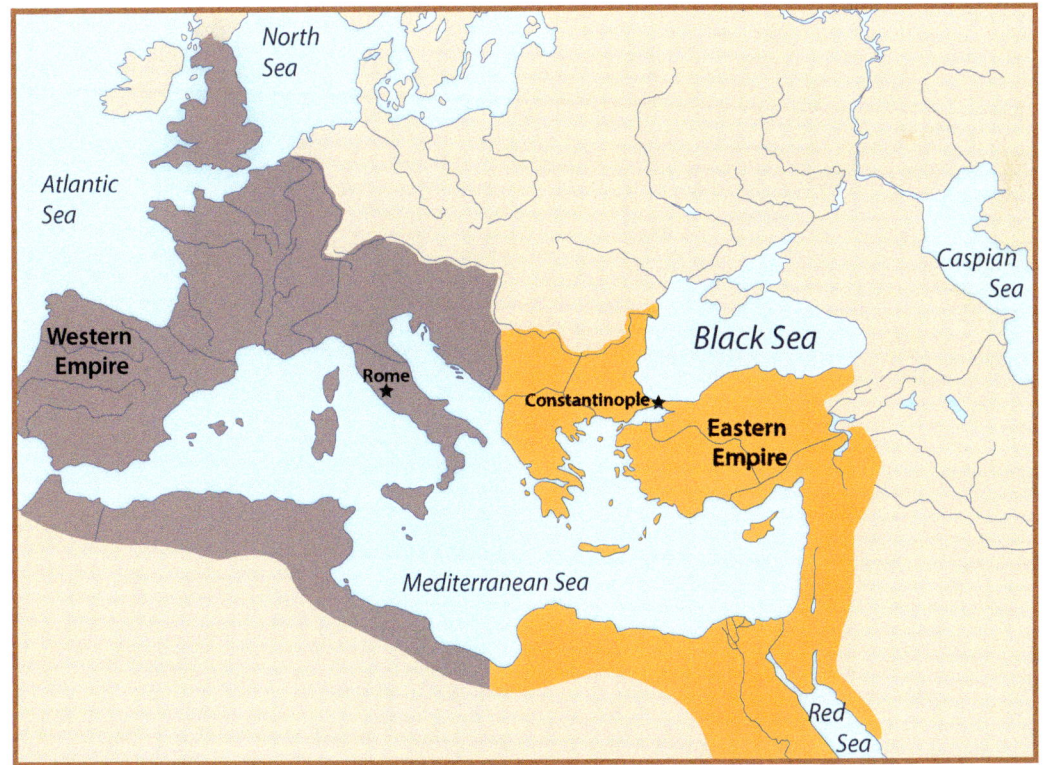

The Roman Empire at its peak

to Latin and making up myths to connect them with the beginnings of their own society. They also liked the looks of the graceful pillars of the Greek temples, so they added them to the arches and domes of their building designs. Augustus was a great patron of art, and he commissioned Roman sculptors to make copies of the natural-looking statues of the Greeks. This was a good thing, too, since many of the Greek statues have been lost and only the copies survive.

Roman copy of a Greek statue

The Greeks invented the theater and wrote the first plays. Does it surprise you that the Romans tried to copy these, too? Plautus, Terrence, and Seneca were Roman playwrights who wrote "updated" versions of Greek plays, although theirs were more melodramatic than the originals. Greece certainly had a civilizing effect upon the ruder, cruder Romans. The model Roman citizen of Augustus' time was a clone of the Greek aristocrat: well-educated, skilled in many disciplines, including sports, and actively involved in politics. These characteristics would later define the ideal "Renaissance Man."

The Empire Is Divided

But nothing lasts forever, and by the third century AD the awesome Roman Empire was in decline. There were many reasons for this, but a major factor was the hordes of barbarian tribesmen who relentlessly threatened the borders in eastern Europe. The Emperor Diocletian decided that his realm was simply too unwieldy to defend, so he divided it into two parts, each with its own ruler. The western section included much of Europe. Its capital was Rome and the official language remained Latin. The eastern part stretched across Greece, Asia Minor, the coast of Asia, and northeastern Africa. Its capital was Constantinople (present day Istanbul) and the official language was Greek. Because Constantinople was built upon the site of the ancient city of Byzantium, the eastern section came to known as the Byzantine Empire.

Christianity became the official religion of the Romans in 395, but eventually the Church,

Dome of the Roman Pantheon

too, split in two. The western empire fell under the auspices of the Roman Catholic Church, headed by the Pope in Rome. People living in the Byzantine Empire were members of the Greek Orthodox Church, whose leader was the Patriarch in Constantinople.

The Fall of Rome

In 476 the last Roman emperor was booted off his throne by invading barbarian warriors, and the efficient Roman government bureaucracy fizzled in the West. Cities were abandoned, roads became over-grown with weeds, and the trading network that had brought prosperity to southern Europe fell apart. Wealthy landowners built thick-walled castles and fought one another over the ownership of land. It was a dangerous era, and no one had much time to think about anything except how to survive. Most people settled in villages near the castles and exchanged their labor in the fields for protection by the knights of the local lord.

This period of history is known as the Middle Ages. The term "Middle Ages" was coined by Renaissance scholars who accepted Petrarch's view that nothing much happened during the years falling "in the middle" of ancient times and their own age. It is true that during those difficult years learning and scholarship were nearly forgotten. But literacy did continue to thrive in monasteries, where monks carefully preserved the books of the past in their libraries and painstakingly made new copies of them to exchange with other monasteries. These books included the works of Roman writers like Cicero and Livy as well as those of the Church Fathers (Catholic theologians such as Saint Augustine). And, of course, the monks made plentiful copies of the Bible, which they elaborately decorated and illustrated.

A monk at work

In the twelfth century knights returned home from the Crusades in the Holy Land. (The Crusades were a series of military campaigns overseen by the Catholic Church to win back Jerusalem and other regions from the Muslim Turks.) The Crusaders had developed a taste for such eastern luxuries as silk and spices. Enterprising merchants in France, Germany, and Italy took advantage of the growing interest in imported products and slowly reestablished a trading network. This offered opportunities for local craftsmen to create articles, such as woven cloth and wooden carvings, that could be exchanged for the eastern goods. This revival of trade encouraged the settlement of new towns. Big changes were brewing, and western Europe had begun to climb out of the dark abyss.

Meanwhile, Muslim invaders gradually carved away huge chunks of the Byzantine Empire, until by the twelfth century it was reduced to the land surrounding Constantinople and a few other outposts. However, the eastern capital continued to prosper as a center of trade, art, learning, and, of course, religion.

The Medieval Mindset

After Rome fell, the Catholic Church had stepped in to replace the crumbling imperial government with its own organization. This was an easy transition, because the framework of the Church administration was modeled upon the bureaucracy that had once governed the sprawling Roman Empire. And since nearly everyone in western Europe was a member of the Church, the Pope became an incredibly powerful man.

The doctrines of the Church influenced nearly aspect of daily living. According to Catholic belief, man was a miserable sinner who was condemned to struggle against all sorts of obstacles in his difficult journey through life. The one thing that sustained him was the hope that his soul might spend eternity in a heavenly paradise after he died. But to stand any chance at all in obtaining salvation (entry into heaven), he needed to carefully adhere to the rigid teachings of the Church, to faithfully participate in the seven holy sacraments (special religious ceremonies, such as daily mass), to make a pilgrimage to a holy shrine, and to confess his sins to the local priest. Should he fail in any of these requirements, or should he be tempted to stray beyond the bounds of piety, his soul might face eternal damnation in hell (a fiery place ruled by the devil himself).

Given this great concern about the afterlife, most people did just what the Church instructed them to do. Their faith was the focus of their lives, and the local priest was their spiritual advisor. Actually, he was more than that. Not only did the priest lead the services, perform the sacraments, and collect the tithes (everyone had to give the Church one tenth of his income), but he also knew everyone's darkest secrets. And because he was often the only person in a town who could read and write, his parishioners depended upon him for advice in most practical matters - everything from interpreting a legal document to deciphering the words in a business contract.

Church spire rises above a medieval town in France

The spire of the local church soared high above the houses and shops in every medieval city, town, and village, reminding the people of their religious obligations. The church bells served as a giant alarm clock, announcing when it was time for work, meals or prayer. (Not surprisingly it was a monk who invented the first mechanical clock.) Parishioners gathered at the church not only for services but to celebrate such special family events as marriage and baptism. They even attended religious plays there called miracles and mysteries.

Medieval church bell

Medieval Scholarship

As we learned earlier, the spark of learning was kept alive in the monasteries, where young monks were taught to read and to make copies of old manuscripts. Beginning in the twelfth century new schools were set up in the cathedrals of the larger cities. These were often attended by boys who had no interest in a career in the Church. They wanted to learn to read, write, and perform mathematical calculations in order to keep records for the growing class of merchants.

Most scholars of this period were priests and monks who studied the writings of the early theologians. Over the centuries, as copies of handwritten manuscripts were copied and recopied, mistakes were inevitably made and then repeated. Inevitably, the scholars noticed inconsistencies and even contradictions among the various versions of a single text. What to do? The solution was to seek out the original Latin works that had been preserved in the monastic libraries.

The Past Collides With the Present

The study of the original writings of Christian theologians led to the reexamination of other ancient works that had little to do with religion. The Romans left behind a great wealth of literary materials, and scholars like Petrarch discovered in them a view of life that differed greatly from that of the Church. The Latin writers celebrated the resourcefulness of the individual and rejoiced in his potential to forge his own destiny. What a contrast to the Catholic portrayal of man as a miserable sinner, a helpless pawn whose life is determined by Divine Will!

Engraving of a pensive scholar

In the twelfth century the writings of Aristotle, a brilliant Greek philosopher, became available in many parts of Europe. Among other things, Aristotle attempted to explain the existence of the universe in purely rational terms. What a shock this must have been for the priestly scholars who were trained to accept everything as a matter of faith! Aristotle's writings inspired many clerics to reexamine their own approach to knowledge and belief. Some, such as Peter Abelard and Thomas Aquinas, used the logic of the Greek to try to justify their religious faith. Their method of using logical arguments to prove the validity of religious doctrine and to reconcile contradictory viewpoints is known as scholasticism. It occupied the minds of many of the finest medieval theologians for a long time. As we will see, certain scholars later accused the scholasticists of becoming so blinded by logical theories that they lost sight of the essence of religious faith. (Can you see how this might happen?)

The original Greek texts of the New Testament also became available in the twelfth century. And guess what! There were numerous contradictions between these and the Latin Vulgate (Saint Jerome's version of the Old Testament which had been the standard Bible of the Church since the fifth century). This discovery reinforced the scholars' determination to return to original sources for all matter of study.

The First Universities

Contrary to Petrarch's scathing words, the people of the Middle Ages did create a number of important things, including the university (although the concept of higher learning had its origins in ancient Greece). The university began as a gathering place for scholars and students who were anxious to share their love of knowledge. In time groups of teachers banded together to form a professional guild, known as a *universitas* (a Latin term meaning "an association of people"). They gave lectures to anyone who could afford

The University of Pisa has existed since medieval times

their fees and they granted degrees, recognized throughout Europe, which served as licenses to teach. From these loose organizations emerged the first major universities in Bologna, Paris, and Oxford. By the thirteenth century many others had sprung up in the larger cities of Europe. Many of these were in Italy, in cities such as

Florence, Rome, Siena, Pisa, Padua, Naples, and Bologna.

The university curriculum was based upon the works of classical (ancient Greek and Roman) authors, not the Church Fathers and the Bible. The students were eager to learn more about the nature of man rather than the relationship between man and God. Because they enrolled in the courses of the *Studia Humanitas* (studies of mankind) that had formed the core of a classical education (grammar, rhetoric, ethics, poetry, history, and philosophy), they came to be known as humanists.

University classes were taught in Latin, the language of the Church and therefore the language of scholarship. (Remember, for centuries the only literate people were the monks and clerics.) For this reason, a knowledge of Latin became the sign of an educated person. The students probably spouted it among the townspeople to flaunt their special status! Books were rare, so teachers would read aloud (these were the original "lectures") while students diligently took notes. They memorized the notes and recited them as perfectly as possible during examinations. Incidentally, in those days university students were younger than modern college students. A boy was eligible to attend a university at the age of twelve, and he might begin graduate studies in law, medicine or theology in his late teens.

The Spread of Humanism

Eventually, all scholars who studied human society, who placed critical thinking over faith, came to be known as humanists. Their desire to learn from original sources inspired them to track down a wider range of ancient texts than had been previously available to learned men. It

seemed like everyone was singing the praises of the great thinkers of the ancient world. In the thirteenth century the Pope became so worried about the way the humanists were embracing Greek logic that he threatened to excommunicate (expel from the Church) any students at the University of Paris who were caught reading anything by Aristotle! But it was impossible to stem the tide.

Statue of Aristotle in Greece

In the fourteenth century Giovanni Aurispa brought two hundred Greek manuscripts from Constantinople to Italy, including the complete works of Plato, Aristotle's teacher. Plato had recorded the ideas of his own mentor, Socrates, in a long series of dialogues, but he also expressed original ideas about how people should be governed. In his opinion, the brightest and most highly educated men made the best rulers because they based their decisions upon rational analysis.

Like many other thinkers of his time, Plato believed that since laws were made by people, they could be changed by people. The Church, on the other hand, had been preaching for centuries that the highest laws were made by God and were therefore permanent and unchangeable. Once again the rational thought of the past was bumping into the faith of the present. Plato had also pondered the meaning of reality, wondering whether something really existed or simply seemed to exist in the mind of an individual.

Armed with ideas gleaned from the ancients, the humanists joyfully embraced the image of man as a rational, self-sufficient individual who could determine for himself what was good or true. Their model was Roman citizen, who divided his time between enriching his scope of knowledge and contributing to the welfare of the government. Compared to this image, contemporary people seemed crude and misdirected. And while the ancients had stressed balance and harmony, the present world seemed to thrive upon chaos and disorder.

Although the humanists sought ways in which people could live fuller, more meaningful lives, they continued to believe in the teachings of the Bible. Most scholars were devout Christians. What had changed was their attitude about the freedom of the individual to mold his own life. The emphasis was upon the "here and now," the natural and secular (non-religious) world, rather than the spiritual afterlife. Along with a new optimism about man's freedom of choice came the assumption that the more a person understood and enjoyed the beauty of life, the greater would be his appreciation of and belief in God. This link between a desire to understand the mysteries of the physical universe and a strong faith in God helped make the ideas of the humanists acceptable to most Catholics.

Everyday Life in Florence

Let's take a close look at Florence, Italy. In the fourteenth century, it was a bustling city whose narrow, twisting streets were lined with several-storied buildings of plastered brick. Stores and workshops were located on the ground floor of many of the structures, while the upper levels contained apartments. These were cramped quarters, and in most cases the kitchen became a bedroom at night, when woven straw mats were placed on the floor. There were no closets, so wooden chests were filled with clothing and packed with bay leaves to keep away the fleas, lice, and bedbugs that seemed to be everywhere. The few windows had no glass (this was much too expensive) but were covered with oiled cloth. At night, a wick in a dish of olive oil provided the only light. Since there was no system of plumbing and sanitation, garbage and human waste were routinely dumped out of windows into the streets, creating an unhealthy (and foul-smelling) environment.

This street in Siena dates back to medieval times

Scattered among the crowded apartment buildings were the large houses of the successful merchants. The typical merchant's dwelling

Bell tower of Palazzo della Signoria

had an enclosed courtyard and a private well, which was a great luxury in those days when most families fetched water from a public fountain. Although it had many rooms, there were no hallways or connecting corridors. To get to his bedroom, a guest might have to pass through several other rooms. This was less of a problem than you might think, since in early times people had less concern for privacy than we do nowadays. Some homes had a primitive toilet - a board with several holes suspended over a stream diverted from the Arno River, flowing through a narrow space between buildings. Most people, however, made do with a chamber pot, which, as we've learned, was emptied into the street.

The *Piazza della Signoria* (Square of the Signoria) was the civic heart of Florence, the setting for political rallies and festivities. It was dominated by the large *Palazzo della Signoria*, a cubical, crenellated building that looks a lot like a fortress. The Palazzo's bells sounded the alarm of an approaching army (calling all men to the city walls and gates) or summoned citizens to the square for a public assembly. (The bell tower has three bells, the oldest one cast in the thirteenth century.) Even today the building, now called the Palazzo Vecchio (Old Palace), continues to function as Florence's town hall.

Sometimes riotous activities took place in the square. On one occasion a man was nearly eaten alive (he was badly bitten) by Florentines who were maddened by his political speech! Another time wild boars and lions were released for citizens to shoot. There are even accounts of wild buffalos being stampeded across the cobblestones - just for fun! The square was also the site of public executions.

Piazza della Signoria

Florence had a number of attractive Gothic churches. The Dominican church of Santa Maria Novella was built in the fourteenth century, although only the lower part of the façade standing today was completed. The upper part would be designed and built in the fifteenth century. Construction of the Franciscan church of Santa Croce was begun in 1294. But the spiritual center of Florence was the cathedral of Santa Maria del Fiore, most of which was completed in the thirteenth century.

Three Literary Giants

Three extraordinary Italian scholars of the fourteenth century - Dante, Petrarch, and Boccaccio - produced the first great literary works that reflected the spirit of humanism. They wrote about secular issues as well as religious ones and dealt with a wide spectrum of human emotions. For them, love and greed were just as interesting as piety. Although they produced scholarly works in Latin, their most memorable books were written in the everyday language of their countrymen (the vernacular). Thanks to them, literature could be enjoyed by anyone who could read, scholar and merchant alike.

Dante

Dante Alighiere (1265-1321) was educated in a cathedral school in Florence and later attended the University of Bologna. He became a brilliant classical scholar and a gifted poet. He met the inspiration of much of his writings at a May Day festival when he was only nine - a lovely young girl known as Beatrice (she was eight). She was dressed in a crimson gown and to young Dante she looked like an angel. It was love at first sight, although they exchanged few words. The girl's

identity is somewhat of a mystery, but many historians believe she was Bice, the daughter of a minor nobleman named Folco Portinari.

Statue of Dante in Florence, Italy

Dante thought about Beatrice constantly and wrote many poems about her. Yet, he didn't encounter her again until nine years later, when he met her as she was strolling with two other girls. Beatrice was dressed in white and seemed to the love-struck Dante like the essence of purity. When she greeted him, he felt as though he had been struck by lightning! Shortly afterward, Beatrice heard some gossip linking Dante with another girl. She was so disturbed (not that she had a right to be) that she passed him on the street without speaking to him. He mourned for days and days! Beatrice later married another man (her marriage was arranged by her parents). She died at the age of twenty-five, but she remained the muse of the poet who loved her so passionately for the rest of his life.

Terracotta statue of Beatrice

Beatrice represented for Dante ideal and unattainable love. His poems about her were influenced by the medieval tradition of courtly love expressed by the troubadour poets of twelfth century France. Those early minstrels had composed verses about the love intrigues between wealthy nobles and attractive married (and thus unobtainable) women of the court. Thirty-one of Dante's poems about Beatrice are contained in his collection, *The New Life*. His lyrical verses are interspersed with prose commentaries describing his great love. The title of the book refers to Dante's decision upon the death of Beatrice to devote the rest of his life to a new passion, philosophy. His beautiful love poems are still enjoyed for their melodic rhythm and unique blending of emotion and logic.

As a young man Dante was actively involved in Florentine politics, but when an opposition party gained power he was exiled from his own city. He made no effort to return, since he was sentenced to be burned alive if caught in Florence! He spent the following years at the courts in several Italian cities, devoting much of his time to studying the works of such classical writers as Virgil, Cicero, Ovid, and Aristotle. He also pondered the views of theologians Saint Augustine and Saint Thomas Aquinas, and he carefully analyzed the Scriptures. These scholarly pursuits led to the creation of his masterpiece, a long narrative poem entitled *The Divine Comedy*, which he began in 1307. It ranks among the finest works of world literature, combining elements of medieval theology with the ideals of the humanists.

The Divine Comedy was written in *terza rima* (triple rhyme), a form Dante invented in which the first and third lines of a tercet (set of three lines) rhyme, while the middle line rhymes with the first and third lines of the next tercet. The language is the vernacular spoken in Tuscany (the region surrounding Florence). Written in the first person, the work describes the poet's imaginary journey through the world of the dead. It is divided into three sections: *Inferno* (Hell), (Purgatory), and *Paradiso* (Heaven). Dante firmly believed in the Christian concept of salvation (admittance into heaven as a reward for leading a moral and pious life). People who sinned against the Divine Law (rules expressed by the Church) would surely end up in a fiery hell, although if they repented for their errors they went to an intermediary place (purgatory) until, through the prayers of living friends and relatives, they had suitably atoned for their sins. Once purified (purged) they ascended into heaven. Remember these basic beliefs about getting into heaven.

They had a tremendous influence upon the artists and writers of the Renaissance.

Given its religious theme, *The Divine Comedy* seems the typical work of a medieval Catholic.

Relief painting of Dante holding his book

But it is also an allegory of mankind's search for a moral and meaningful life. And on yet another level, it is a satire of the society of fourteenth century Italy, filled with vivid (and often damning) portraits of well-known political leaders, poets, and philosophers of the time.

Here's the plot. With the Roman poet Virgil as his guide, Dante leaves the "dark wood" of his middle age and passes through the gates of Hell, descending through the nine circles of the damned. Hell is described as a huge, funnel-shaped pit located directly beneath the holy city of Jerusalem. Its nine circles are a series of terraces, each one of lesser circumference than the one above. Each circle is designated for a specific sin, the lesser sins near the top and the more terrible ones at the bottom. Punishments correspond to the type of sins committed. As he and Virgil descend, Dante sees thieves struggling in a pit of snakes and demons, murderers perpetually drowning in a river of blood, and flatterers swimming in a canal of excrement! He observes fortune-tellers whose heads are reversed on their bodies so they have to walk backwards forever. (Why is this an appropriate punishment?) The worst sinners of all are the traitors, who are confined to a frozen lake. In the center of the lake, Judas, Brutus, and Cassius (history's three worst traitors) are eternally being crushed by the teeth of Lucifer (the devil).

The suffering souls Dante observes in Hell are in fact caricatures of contemporaries whom he personally knew or knew about. He clearly enjoyed assigning punishments to men he considered greedy or dishonest - especially greedy moneylenders and self-indulgent popes. He consigned the ancient authors to the first circle, known as the "State of Limbo" which was designated for the virtuous but unbaptized. (The writers had lived before Christianity became the state religion of Rome.) Their only punishment is to be deprived of the vision of God.

From the rim of Hell the two poets climb through a narrow passageway to the shore of the mountain island of Purgatory. They ascend seven terraces where the seven major vices are purged. For example, the eyes of the envious are sewn shut. At the top of the mountain is the "Terrestrial Paradise," which Adam and Eve had to leave because of their sins. (Their happy existence ended when Eve tempted Adam with a forbidden fruit, an apple.) Here Dante is joined by his beloved Beatrice, and together they ascend into the heavens to meet the souls of the blessed at the outermost of ten concentric heavenly spheres. This is the abode of God, the angels and the saints.

Dante's journey through the afterlife can easily be interpreted as the common man's journey through this life. With the aid of his reason (represented by Virgil) a person can understand the evils of immoral behavior, take steps to deal with his own failings, and ultimately find happiness and fulfillment. Dante's masterful blending of the values of the pagan world of classical antiquity with those of Christianity make *The Divine Comedy* an important link between the Middle Ages and the Renaissance.

Petrarch

Dante was the literary hero of the Italian poet we already met in the prologue of this book: Francesco Petrarca, known as Petrarch (1304-1374). He was born in Arezzo, Italy, but he spent his early years in Avignon, France. Petrarch studied law at the University of Bologna, where he also distinguished himself as a gifted classical scholar and a talented poet.

Statue of Petrarch in Florence, Italy

Petrarch's interest in the ancient world prompted him to search for original manuscripts tucked away in French and Italian monasteries, and he encouraged his friends to bring to him any that they found. His greatest discovery was a collection of letters written by Roman authors Cicero and Livy. He read these over and over again until he felt that he actually knew those thoughtful men who had lived over a thousand years earlier. In fact, he wrote letters back to them! In one, he thanked Livy for enabling him to forget the evils of the present and transporting him back to happier, better times. Once he pretended that Cicero visited him in France and wrote about their exchange of views! Petrarch built up an excellent classical library and made it available to other scholars. About forty-four surviving manuscripts of his personal collection have been identified.

Like most humanists, Petrarch considered ancient Rome to be the heart of western civilization, and he felt that its legacy of literature, philosophy, art, politics, and law had been ignored for too long. Of course, theologians had been reading Latin texts for centuries, and more recently scholasticists were applying Aristotle's logic to justify their own religious views. But Petrarch was among the first to propose that the culture of the classical world should be studied in its own right. He didn't view the Romans as the musty figures of a dead past but rather as fascinating men and women who came alive through their words in the ancient manuscripts. As we've learned, Petrarch had no problem communicating with them, and he believed they were equally approachable to others who were willing to make the effort.

Like other humanists, he greatly admired the Roman concept of a virtuous citizen who felt a sense of responsibility to develop his talents as an individual and to use these talents to enrich the community in which he lived. He hoped that as scholars rediscovered the writings of the Romans, they would break through the darkness of their times and recapture the brilliance of antiquity.

Petrarch wrote many notes and letters (including the fictional epistles to his classical heroes) expressing his deepest feelings about friendship, love, and nature. His greatest work was *The Book of Songs* - a collection of 366 poems inspired by his unrequited (unreturned) love for a young golden-haired woman he called Laura. He first saw Laura on April 6, 1327, in the Church of Santa Clara in Avignon, France. He immediately fell in love with her. (Does this remind you of Dante's obsession with Beatrice?) Her refusal to return his love inspired his greatest lyric poems. Petrarch compared Laura to Daphne, the lovely nymph in Greek mythology whose love was vainly sought by the god Apollo. (To escape his embrace, she turned into a laurel tree.) Little is known of Laura, but we do know that she died in the terrible plague of 1348. She expired twenty-one years to the day Petrarch first saw her in church.

Although he wrote his prose in Latin, Petrarch followed Dante's lead and composed his love poems in the vernacular of Tuscany. They represent a refinement of the lyric tradition of the troubadours, combining elegance and clarity with a sense of wistful melancholy. Most of the poems are sonnets. Petrarch did not invent the sonnet (it has fourteen lines with rhymes arranged according to a certain pattern), but his poems are so beautifully written that this form became the major genre of the poets writing in the fifteenth and sixteenth centuries.

Petrarch traveled widely and was popular in courts throughout Europe for his humanist ideas as well as his evocative poetry. In 1341 he was crowned poet laureate in Rome, the first to be so honored since ancient times. He spent the last six years of his life near Padua, Italy and died peacefully, surrounded by his Latin manuscripts.

During his last months he wrote a letter about himself, addressed to later generations. It describes his major ambitions and ends with the words, "I strove to forget the present and join myself in spirit with the past." In so doing, he helped set the tone for the future.

Boccaccio

Giovanni Boccaccio (1313-75) was born in Florence and went to Naples as a young man to learn about the trading business from the wealthy Bardi family. While in Naples he became friendly with a circle of humanists, who encouraged him to turn aside from the business career his father had intended for him in favor of scholarship.

Statue of Boccaccio in Florence

Like Dante and Petrarch, whom he greatly admired, Boccaccio was drawn to the richness of classical literature. He actually met Petrarch in 1530, and the two formed a friendship that endured until the older man's death. Boccaccio followed the lead of Dante and Petrarch in another way: he fell in love with a woman he could not marry. The object of his affections was Fiammetta (possibly the daughter of King Robert of Anjou). Like Beatrice and Laura, Fiammetta inspired his love poetry.

Boccaccio also composed pastoral allegories, heroic versions of myths, prose romances, novellas, a psychological novel (he invented this form), epic poems in rhyme, and numerous short lyrics. His best-known work is *The Decameron*, a bawdy collection of 100 short tales about contemporary Italian life. In the introduction of the book we meet three young men and seven young women who have fled to the countryside to escape the plague that has invaded the cities. They decide to entertain each other with stories, which they share each hot afternoon. Every story has a different theme, and together they present a portrait of every level of the Florentine society of Boccaccio's day. The stories are written in prose in the Tuscan vernacular. (Boccaccio is considered the first great writer of prose in a modern language.) *The Decameron* takes its name from the Greek word for ten, since the tales are told over a period of ten days. It was extremely popular among educated Italians - try to envision them sitting around a banquet table laughing about a colorful episode. Of course, the Pope found the book shocking and forbade any Catholic to read it.

Fresco of a scene from The Decameron

Boccaccio devoted his later years to searching for ancient texts in Naples and at the Benedictine Abbey in Monte Cassino. He also found time to master the Greek language as well as classical history, literature, and mythology. He even produced a huge encyclopedia of ancient mythology, *Families of the Gods*.

He wrote an affectionate biography of Dante, and in 1373 the Florentine government invited him to deliver a series of public readings of *The Divine Comedy*. In that same year he met Geoffrey Chaucer, the author of *The Canterbury Tales*. Chaucer was the first English writer to compose literary works in the English vernacular, so the two men must have had much to discuss. Boccaccio died eighteen months after Petrarch. At the time of his death Florentine writer Franco Sacchetti remarked, "All poetry is now extinct."

The Italian Language Is Reformed

The heritage of the ancient past clearly molded the creative geniuses of Dante, Petrarch, and Boccaccio, but this legendary trio had to look within their souls to produce their extraordinary literary works. Their achievements had a profound effect upon those who lived after them. Not only did they launch a literary movement based upon the ideals of humanism, but they made the vernacular just as respectable as Latin for the written page.

Before their time, there was no standard language in Italy (apart from the Latin of scholars and priests). Every region had its own distinct dialect. But *The Divine Comedy*, *The Book of Songs*, and *The Decameron* were so widely read that the Tuscan dialect became familiar throughout the Italian peninsula. By the fifteenth century it was spoken by every well-educated Italian, and in time it would evolve into the language of modern Italy.

Review Questions

1. Describe the two parts of the Roman Empire. How were they similar? How were they different?

2. Which part of the empire lasted longer (western or eastern)?

3. What was the Catholic belief about the afterlife?

4. Why did medieval scholars first start looking for original manuscripts?

5. What is scholasticism?

6. How did humanism differ from medieval theology?

7. What are the three books of Dante's *Divine Comedy*?

8. What are some of the interpretations of Dante's epic poem?

9. Why is Petrarch considered a humanist?

10. In what major way did Petrarch influence Boccaccio?

11. In what language were the major works of the "talented trio" of fourteenth century Italy written?

12. Who were the three ladies who inspired these poets?

Further Thoughts

1. Latin had evolved since the days of ancient Rome. The scholars of the Renaissance decided they wanted to write only in the "pure" Latin of Cicero (who lived in the first century BC). Their attempts to maintain Ciceronian Latin "froze" the language and prevented any further change in its structure. Eventually, only scholars and Catholic clergymen were fluent in Latin, so it became a "dead" language. Nonetheless, Latin is still taught in many schools today, partly because nearly one half of all English words are derived from that ancient tongue.

2. The humanists weren't the first to appreciate ancient times. The Frankish king Charlemagne was crowned in 800 as ruler of the Roman Empire in Europe. He used the Roman form of government, encouraged the growth of monasteries, and showed great interest in classical learning. Unfortunately, after he died his vast territory was split up and most of his ideals were (temporarily) forgotten.

3. The revival of Greek learning in the West was stimulated when scholar Manuel Chrysoloras was invited to Florence from Constantinople in 1395. Italian scholars knew Latin well, but few in Italy had studied Greek. Chrysoloras remained only a few years in Florence, teaching Greek, and then he moved on to teach in Bologna and later in Venice and Rome. A group of his best students remained a close-knit group. They actively promoted the revival of Greek studies in Italy.

4. The number three has a special significance in Dante's *Divine Comedy*. Perhaps this is because a central concept of Christian theology is the trinity (Father, Son, and Holy Ghost). Dante's poem is divided into three sections, there are nine levels of Hell (a multiple of three), and numerous other examples of the poet's use of this religiously significant number. But it's important to know that three was also a magic number with the ancients - the Greeks had three graces (goddesses of beauty, personifying beauty, charm, and grace) and nine muses (goddesses associated with the arts, including music, lyric poetry, comedy, tragedy, and dance).

5. Dante was greatly influenced by Aristotle's *Ethics* when he wrote *The Divine Comedy*. He once remarked that Aristotle was "the master of those who know."

6. When Petrarch was very old and dying, his friend Boccaccio advised him to take it easy and to stop writing. The older poet responded that he had to keep on, because his writing might be useful to "others far away, perhaps even those who will be born a thousand years from now." No doubt his influence will live on until the twenty-fourth century, and beyond!

7. In the sixteenth century Venetian poet Pietro Bembo would start a vogue for imitations of Petrarch. His *Prose of the Vernacular* set out proposals for a standardized language and style in Italy, using Petrarch and Boccaccio as his models.

Projects

1. In a much modified form, the ideals of the humanists survive in the study of the "humanities" in our modern universities. Find out specifically what is meant today by the humanities.

2. Reread the description of Dante's vision of Hell and then make a diagram of it. It might be helpful to check out the information available in your library or online to obtain a more detailed idea of the various levels.

3. Obtain a copy of *The Divine Comedy*. Choose a colorful passage and read it aloud to your class.

4. Petrarch was fascinated by the writings of Cicero and Livy. Select one of these two Roman writers and find out about his life and his works. Then write a short report. Be sure to explain why Petrarch liked this writer so much.

5. Petrarch's sonnets about his love for Laura became the model for love poetry for centuries to come. Obtain a copy of his poems and read at least three of them.

6. Petrarch compared Laura to Daphne (and himself to Apollo). Find a book of Greek mythology and read the myth about Daphne and Apollo. Then explain how Apollo's infatuation with Daphne compares to Petrarch's love for Laura.

7. Boccaccio wrote *The Decameron* at the time of the Black Death. Find out more about this deadly occurrence and write a short report.

8. Among the early admirers and imitators of Dante was Geoffrey Chaucer, who wrote *The Canterbury Tales*. Obtain a copy of this book from your library. Read the introduction and then enjoy a few of the tales. Think about the ways in which Chaucer was influenced by Dante. Write a paragraph expressing your views.

9. Pretend that Beatrice, Laura and Fiammetta encounter one another in heaven. Imagine the stories they could share! Write a short skit based upon their conversations. It can be funny!

Notre Dame Cathedral, Paris

CHAPTER 2

ARTISTIC AWAKENINGS

The Catholic Church so dominated medieval society that the Middle Ages are known as the Age of Faith. The art and architecture of the period reflect this preoccupation with religion. Magnificent stone cathedrals reach toward the heavens with their soaring spires and high arches, while elongated statues depict saints and biblical figures. The emphasis is upon the majesty of God and the spiritual qualities of the holy people associated with Christianity.

Renaissance scholars referred to the medieval style of architecture and art as Gothic - a word derived from the Goths, barbarians who helped bring about the fall of Rome. They considered it unrefined and primitive when compared to the art of classical Greece and Rome. Times have certainly changed. Today Gothic buildings and figures are admired for their grace and beauty.

Statues of saints, Notre Dame Cathedral

Gothic Art

You might find medieval paintings rather unrealistic. It would be difficult to imagine actually speaking to the static, other-worldly figures or walking through the decorative landscapes that are gilded with gold leaf and often strewn with symbolic objects. Even the size of the people varies in an unnatural way. The principal figures are quite large and centrally placed, while less important ones appear small and are sometimes even squeezed into a corner for lack of space.

Medieval painting of St. Francis

Byzantine Architecture and Art

The Italian artists of the Middle Ages were influenced by the styles of the Byzantine Empire. This is partly because Italian merchants were able to observe first-hand the extraordinary buildings in Constantinople and then return home with enthusiastic accounts of what they had seen.

Hagia Sophia

Byzantine icon of Madonna and Jesus

Italy, soon after the Hagia Sophia. It is the largest and best preserved Byzantine church outside of Constantinople.

The interiors of Byzantine churches are decorated with mosaic pictures and designs. These are made from small pieces of colored stone or glass fitted and cemented together. As in the Gothic paintings, the figures are stiff and stylized. (To stylize is to represent something according to a pattern rather than according to nature.) Madonnas (portraits of the Virgin Mary) lack naturalistic detail or any sense of movement, and

Sometimes Byzantine artists and architects came to Italy to design and decorate churches. The typical Byzantine church is very different from the Gothic cathedrals. First of all, it has a large central dome, a feature inherited from the Romans. The dome is in the center of the four equal arms of a Greek cross. The magnificent church of Hagia Sophia (Holy Wisdom) in Constantinople (built in the sixth century) is considered the finest example of early Byzantine architecture. It was converted into a mosque in the fifteenth century, and today it is a museum.

The octagonal church of San Vitale, which is of Byzantine design, was built in Ravenna,

San Vitale

because there is no natural setting all the figures possess a spiritual quality and seem to drift about, unencumbered by any earthly bonds. Byzantine paintings are equally unrealistic. Every figure faces forward and is set apart from the others (except, of course, Mary, who holds the baby Jesus).

Mosaics in San Vitale

And yet, the eastern figures are not totally lifeless. Since the Byzantine Empire was a storehouse of Greek culture, the local artists had ready access to the natural-looking classical paintings and statues. They incorporated into their own pictures many of the features of the ancient works, such as the graceful folds of clothing (which they represented with lines), modeling of the faces, and even, on occasion, foreshortening of an arm (distorting the arm to make it seem to be projecting forward). These attempts to introduce an element of realism were a harbinger of things to come.

Drama Captured in Stone

An early glimmer of the lifelike statues of the Renaissance appears in the works of Italian sculptor Nicola Pisano (1220-84). Pisano was inspired by the relief statues on the Roman sarcophagi (stone coffins) that had been brought by crusading knights to Pisa (Italy) from the Holy Land. (A relief statue is cut out of a stone background and appears to stand apart from it.) Pisano had many excellent examples of Roman art to study as the ancient ruins literally littered the countryside around Pisa.

Pisano devoted most of his artistic career to carving the many-sided marble pulpits in Pisa's baptistery (a small building where group baptisms took place) and Siena's cathedral. He set new standards for decorating pulpits with action-filled relief panels. Like the stained-glass windows of Gothic cathedrals, the panels of the pulpits were originally intended to teach illiterate parishioners the stories of the Bible. But Pisano's figures are so lifelike that they can be appreciated for their

Mosaic of Byzantine Emperor Justinian, San Vitale

artistic value alone. In each scene the sculptor has skillfully captured a moment in time, inviting us to sense the unfolding drama and to feel personally involved in the action. This close relationship between the viewer and a work of art had not existed for centuries.

The six panels of the hexagonal Pisa pulpit represent the life of Jesus. Although the figures are crowded together (more than one event is depicted on each panel), they are believable men and women, not drifting phantoms. The influence of the classical sculptures is evident in the folds of draped clothing, which clearly suggest the rounded forms of the human bodies beneath them.

Relief figures on a Roman sarcophagus

Pisano's pulpit in Pisa

Above the panels are statues that symbolize Christian virtues. Pisano modeled the muscular figure of Fortitude on an ancient sculpture of the mythical hero Hercules that he had seen carved on the Roman sarcophagus at Pisa. Similarly, his Virgin Mary was inspired by the goddess Phaedra on that same tomb. By combining the symbolic images of the Christian tradition with the lifelike figures of classical art, and then adding a bit of drama, Pisano broke ground for a whole new style of sculpture.

Giovanni Pisano (1248-1314) was trained as a sculptor by his father, Nicola. Father and son are known by art historians as the Pisani. Giovanni carved sibyls (pagan prophets of antiquity) and Old Testament heroes in the facade of the cathedral of Siena. His figures seem agitated and frenzied, nearly bursting with passionate feelings. The figures he sculpted on the pulpit in the cathedral in Pistoia stand in natural poses, making dramatic gestures. They are filled with emotion. His statues of the Madonna and Child radiate gentleness and love.

The steps involved in painting a fresco were carefully described in the early fifteenth century by Tuscan painter, Cennino Cennini, in his *Book About Art.* Here's how it was done. First a coat of rough plaster *arriccio* was applied to a stone or brick wall. This would smooth the surface and act as a moisture barrier between the wall and the painting. The plaster was a mixture of lime, water, and fine sand (one part lime to three parts sand). When it was dry, the artist dipped a string in charcoal or wet paint, held one end, and snapped it against the wall. The strings made vertical and horizontal guidelines which would help him center the painting and align its various parts.

Next he made a preparatory drawing with a charcoal stick. After 1450 this step was replaced by the use of paper cartoons (stencil-like drawings): The artist drew the figures to be painted on a large

Closeup of a panel

Giovanni had great talent and he knew it. Unlike his predecessors, who never dreamed of taking credit for their accomplishments, he carved on the pulpit of Pistoia the following words: "Giovanni carved it, who performed no empty work. The son of Nicola and blessed with higher skill. Pisa gave him birth and endowed him with mastery greater than any before him." So much for humility!

Frescoes

In the late thirteenth century many Italian painters began to work in a medium known as fresco. A fresco is a painting executed on wet plaster. (In Italian the word "fresco" refers to the wet, freshly plastered wall.) Actually, this was not a new technique - frescoes were painted in ancient times - but the process had long been forgotten. With the revival of interest in classical antiquity, frescoes became extremely popular once again.

Relief carving by Giovanni Pisano

sheet of paper and then pricked hundreds of tiny holes around the outlines of the figures. He then held the cartoon over the plaster and blew charcoal dust through the pinpricks to transfer the outlines onto the wet surface. Then he joined up the dotted lines. Once the preparatory drawing was on the wall, the artist took a brush dipped in water and *sinopia* (a red iron oxide pigment from Sinope on the Black Sea) and retraced the lines. When the sinopia was dry, he brushed off the underlying charcoal with a feather. Now he could begin the actual painting.

Ancient Roman fresco, Pompeii

He added a second coat of finer plaster (*intonaco*) to a small patch called a *giornato* (an Italian word referring to the amount of work that could be completed in a single day). Then he rapidly retraced the outline of the drawing he had covered up with the fine plaster, using the cartoon or the remaining sinopia drawings as a guide. He began painting at the top of the fresco and worked down, so that any drips would fall on the *arriccio* and not on the *intonaco*. Every day he would work on a new giornato until the entire painting was completed. Today, using infrared lighting, we can actually see the outlines of each giornato in an early fresco.

The paint consisted of different colored minerals, ground into a fine powder and mixed with water. As the plaster dried, carbon dioxide was absorbed from the air, converting the lime to calcium carbonate. This crystallized around the sand particles, binding them to the wall. When the paint was applied to the wet plaster, the carbonization process included the particles of pigment. This permanently fixed the colors and made them resistant to further action by water. Fresco was an unforgiving medium: once the pigment was brushed onto the wet plaster it was absorbed immediately and could not easily be erased or altered. To correct a mistake the artist had to cover over a section and start anew. It was a race against time! This is why the artist worked on one small section at a time. The sense of urgency encouraged the artist to make quick strokes which added a sense of life and spontaneity not seen in other medieval paintings.

Of course, not all paintings were frescoes. The altarpiece was a wooden panel (made of small planks of poplar glued together) or a folding set

A fresco in a Gothic church in France

of panels that became an important part of the church interior in the thirteenth century. Often the carved frames were very ornate. The Madonna and Child were often depicted on the main panel, painted quite large so that they could be seen by the entire congregation. To paint an altarpiece, an artist first sanded the panel to make a smooth surface and covered it with several layers of size, a glue made from animal skins. When this was dry, he coated it with *gesso* (fine plaster mixed with glue) as a ground for the under-drawing. When the under-drawing was complete, the background areas were covered with a reddish clay to which were applied pieces of gold leaf. (Gold leaf was made by pounding gold into sheets that were paper thin.) The gold leaf symbolized the purity of heavenly spirits. The figures were then painted with a fine brush. The paint, called tempera, was made from the powdered pigments of ground minerals that were mixed ("tempered") with diluted egg yolk. It dried in a short period of time, since no one knew how to keep the egg yolk from hardening paintings and mosaics.

The Artist's Workshop

By the fourteenth century, most Italian paintings were produced by groups of artists associated with particular workshops. Each workshop was run by a master artist who obtained commissions for his group. The apprentices would grind minerals to make paint, clean palettes and brushes, and prepare wooden panels. Once these duties were seen to they were able to concentrate on learning the techniques of painting. After completing an apprenticeship, a young artist became an assistant. At this stage he could apply the outline sketch or cartoons of a fresco and paint

in the background as well as some details of a work. The master, however, did the main parts of a painting, such as the faces of the major figures. Many assistants became specialists, some being very good at hands and feet, others at clothing, and others at natural backgrounds.

The artists belonged to professional guilds, which drew up contracts with their clients to indicate the theme of a painting as well as the number of people to be included and the specific colors to be used. Many of these contracts have survived, and they tell us much about how paintings were planned and executed in those early times.

An altarpiece

Cimabue

Cenni di Pepa (1240-1302), known as Cimabue (meaning "bull-headed" – he was very stubborn!), accomplished with a paintbrush what Nicola and Giovanni Pisano had with a mallet and chisel. Although he was influenced by medieval and Byzantine art, his figures appear more natural and lifelike. The narrative scenes in his cycle of frescoes in the Church of San Francesco at Assisi reflect his exceptional skill in creating a sense of drama. The crucifix that originally hung above the altar in the Florentine church of Santa Croce in Florence has been attributed to him. The lifeless, limp body of Christ fills you with a sense of pity and sorrow. Although, this work was badly damaged in the flood that ravaged the city of Florence in 1966, it has been fully restored.

According to legend, Cimabue once passed through a small village and noticed a shepherd boy sketching the head of a goat on a rock with a piece of slate. He was so impressed with the boy's talent that he offered to teach him to paint in his workshop. Not long afterward, the young apprentice painted a fly on the face of a figure Cimabue was drawing. The insect was so lifelike that the artist tried to brush it away! Who was this talented young fellow? His name was Ambrogiotto di Bondone (1267-1337), but he is known to us as Giotto.

Fresco by Cimabue of Madonna and Child with Saints, Church of San Francesco, Assisi

Giotto Blazes A New Trail

Giotto admired the relief statues of the Pisani and wondered if he could paint figures that were as life-like and convincing. But creating the illusion of the third dimension (depth) is a difficult thing to do on a two dimensional surface (a painting has only length and width). Giotto solved the problem by adopting from Byzantine art the techniques of foreshortening and shading to create solid-looking figures. He also used lighting to suggest the roundness of a figure or object by illuminating one side and then painting the other side in a shadow. He further heightened the sense of realism by placing his people in natural settings in the Tuscan countryside.

After completing his apprenticeship, Giotto was commissioned to paint a series of frescoes about the life of Saint Francis on the walls of a new church built in the saint's honor in Assisi. He

based most of his figures on the ordinary people he passed in the street, but he hired a local man to pose for the portrait of Francis. Because the eye and mouth are so expressive, he emphasized these features. He arranged his figures so that they seemed to be directly involved in the drama of the scene. One of his most celebrated works is his fresco of the death of Saint Francis in the church of Santa Croce in Florence. Anyone viewing this moving portrait of the dying man surrounded by a group of grieving monks cannot help but sense the brothers' sadness and loss.

Giotto's major work was the series of frescoes painted on the walls of the Arena Chapel for the wealthy merchant, Enrico Scrovegni of Padua. Scrovegni hoped that by building and decorating the chapel he could atone for the sins of his father Reginaldo, a notorious moneylender. (Dante placed the elder Scrovegni in one of the circles of Hell!) In his painting of *The Last Judgment*, Giotto depicted Enrico among the virtuous, handing his chapel to

Death of St Francis, Santa Croce, Florence

piece of paper. Nothing more. The envoy was embarrassed to deliver this "drawing" to the Pope, but when Benedict saw the perfectly executed circle, he was impressed by Giotto's keen eye and absolute control of his paintbrush. By the way, the artist got the job.

Giotto traveled widely and found work in many Italian cities. He was also a shrewd businessman, who invested his profits in the weaving industry of his home town, Mugello (which lies on the outskirts of Florence). He dabbled in architecture, and as a result of this interest he was appointed the Director of Public Works in Florence. He designed the delicate and richly decorated bell tower (campanile) for the city's cathedral, Santa Maria

the Three Marys, while the other moneylenders are shown hanging by the strings of their money bags among the sinners. The other frescoes depict the lives of Mary and Jesus simply, poignantly, and realistically. In viewing the Kiss of Judas, for example, you can sense the action. Judas, the traitor, had told the Roman soldiers that he would identify Jesus by kissing him. The followers of Jesus react (Peter cuts off the ear of a Roman soldier!), while his enemies seem to be out for blood. Giotto has draped his figures in heavy cloth, and through his skillful use of light he has given us a sense of their physiques. He has created a third dimension.

Pope Benedict XI wanted some paintings for the Basilica of Saint Peter in Rome, so he sent an envoy to find out what Giotto's work was like. When the man asked Giotto for a drawing he could take back to Rome, the artist took a brush and drew a circle on a

The Kiss of Judas, Scrovegni Chapel, Padua

del Fiore. It is known today as "Giotto's Tower". Although only the lowest portion was finished at the time of his death, he left behind a model so that it could be completed by several of his pupils.

Giotto's Tower

Giotto was one of the first artists to become famous in his own lifetime. His friend Dante heralded him as the greatest living artist in *The Divine Comedy*. Boccaccio later praised him for bringing the art of painting back to life after centuries of darkness, remarking in *The Decameron*, "Giotto's art was of such excellence that there was nothing in nature that his paintbrush could not exactly reproduce, not simply to make a likeness, but to be the very thing itself. His work was so perfect that a man standing before it would often find his visual senses confused, taking for real what was only painted."

Giotto died in 1337 and was buried in the Cathedral in Florence, a great honor bestowed only upon the most respected and beloved of citizens. Above his tomb is the epitaph, "I am the man who brought painting to life...whatever is found in nature may be found in my art."

Soon after Giotto's death, the terrible plague known as the Black Death arrived in Europe, transmitted by the fleas of infected rats. This was the plague that killed Petrarch's beloved Laura and drove the people in *The Decameron* from the city. By 1353 over one third of the European population had died. This catastrophe set back the development of painting for nearly a century, as artists, worried that God might be punishing humanity for straying from medieval traditions, embraced the guidelines of Gothic art. They created lots of stiff ghostly-looking men and women. But in time, Giotto's lifelike figures and dramatic scenes would inspire new generations of artists to portray humanity in a more believable manner.

Statue of Giotto, Florence

Review Questions

1. Describe a typical Gothic painting.

2. How did Byzantine art differ from Gothic art?

3. How do Nicola Pisano's statues reflect the spirit of humanism?

4. Why was it unusual for Giovanni Pisano to sign his name to a work?

5. Why was a fresco considered a "permanent" painting?

6. What are *giornate*?

7. What is Cimabue's most famous surviving work of art?

8. In what way was Giotto influenced by the Pisani?

9. In what way was he influenced by Byzantine art?

10. What are three ways in which Giotto's works differ from traditional medieval paintings?

Further Thoughts

1. Giotto's contemporary was Duccio di Buoninsegna of Siena. Known as Duccio, he was active 1278-1319. Duccio combined the bold linear styles, splendid coloring, and intricate surface patterns of Byzantine art with a feeling of the human presence. Like Giotto, he placed emphasis on the shape of his figures. Duccio's great altarpiece in the Siena Cathedral, *The Maestra*, focuses on Mary and the holy child. Giotto actually made a trip to Siena (it was a day's journey by horseback from Florence) and was very impressed by the painting. In later years Sienese painters would return the compliment by adopting the realism and naturalism of Giotto.

2. The paints of earth shades such as reds and browns came from clay high in iron. Sometimes the artists used costly minerals to create bright colors. The most highly prized color was a deep blue made by grinding lapus lazuli, a very expensive stone imported from Afghanistan. It was more costly than gold.

Projects

1. Search the Internet for a typical Byzantine painting from the thirteenth century. Print it. Then find a good image of the relief figures of one of the Pisani (father or son). Print it. Closely study the two images. What are the similarities between the two works of art? What are the differences? How does the medieval statue make you feel? How about the Pisano sculpture? Write a short report expressing your observations.

2. Search the Internet for a typical medieval religious painting. Then find an image of a fresco by Giotto. Compare the two styles. Then write a paragraph or two explaining why Giotto's name is associated with humanism.

3. Giotto painted several scenes from the life of Saint Francis of Assisi. Who was the famous holy man? Find out about his life and write a few paragraphs describing what you've learned.

Siena Cathedral

CHAPTER 3

THE ITALIAN CITY-STATES

Now that we know something about the beginnings of Renaissance literature and art, let's take a closer look at Italian society. After the fall of Rome, most of the people of northern Italy lived in small villages. (This was also the case in other parts of western Europe.) The heritage of ancient Rome was visible in every corner of the Italian peninsula. The landscape was peppered with ancient ruins, and nearly every city and village had something - the remains of a temple, a statue, an aqueduct, or even a section of ancient pavement - to remind the local people of Italy's glorious past. These ruins fostered a sense of patriotism, and they helped spark the humanists' campaign to revive the values of the "good old days."

The Growth of Italian Trade

Certain coastal cities took advantage of their strategic locations to carry on a very lucrative maritime trade with ports in the East, particularly Constantinople. The Italian merchants acquired luxury items, such as spices, silk, and jewelry, and shipped them home, where they were sold to other merchants at a good profit. Most of the luxury items, along with locally produced wine and olive oil, were then transported from Italy by wagon through the Alps into France and Germany. There they were traded for northern products, like timber, metals, fish, and wool. The wool was highly sought after by weaving establishments in many cities in Italy. The Italian weavers produced fine woolen cloth that was soon in great demand among the wealthy classes of western Europe.

At first, descendants of the upper class Romans of northern Italy lived near the towns in order to control the local trade and industry, but slowly an expanding middle class of tradesmen began to rival the nobility in wealth and political power. It was this emerging middle class that would eventually fund the great works of art produced during the Italian Renaissance.

Independence and Rivalry

Although northern Italy was officially a part of the Holy Roman Empire (which also included much of modern Germany, Austria, and eastern France), many of its cities gradually obtained self-rule. An independent city and the territory surrounding it became known as a city-state. Like a small kingdom, it raised its own taxes, built its own defenses, and made its own laws. When the Emperor Frederick I threatened to bring northern Italy under tighter control in the twelfth century, sixteen of the city-states formed the Lombard League, which was backed and supported by the Pope. (He didn't want Frederick on his doorstep!) In 1176 the League defeated the Emperor's army, and when Emperor Frederick II renewed the struggle to control northern Italy in the following century, he was also rebuffed. This shows that the city-states could unite if they had to, although they went their separate ways again after Frederick II died.

This conflict between the city-states and the Emperor had led to a division of loyalties among the northern Italians. Some actually supported the policies of the Emperor and felt that he should control the region, while others favored the Italian alliance led by the Pope. This resulted in the creation of two political factions: the *Ghibellines* (supporters of the Emperor) and the *Guelfs* (supporters of the Pope). These factions continued to exist long after the death of Frederick II and had an important effect upon the internal politics of the city of Florence, as we will see.

Florence's cathedral, Santa Maria del Fiore, as we learned earlier, were laid a few decades later.

The spirit of rivalry thrived even within individual communities. An example of this was the race to build the tallest bell tower (campanile). Large numbers of them were constructed in the larger cities, often within view of each other. Some towers reached a height of 200 feet! In San Gimignano no fewer than seventy-six towers were built, of which thirteen survive to this day. In 1250 a law was enacted there limiting a campanile to ninety-six feet, but by that time the public interest had shifted to other matters.

Cathedral and Tower of Pisa

The Italian people were fiercely loyal to their city-states. A person didn't consider himself an Italian; he was a Florentine, a Venetian, a Sienese, or the citizen of some other city. This local pride was reflected in the competition that raged for centuries among the city-states to construct the finest churches. Pisa built a vast religious complex in the late eleventh century that drew visitors from far and wide. (Unfortunately, the marble bell tower was built on an unstable foundation, and it has been leaning ever since.) The majestic cathedral of Siena was completed in 1264, and the foundations of

The Major Powers in Italy

In the early fifteenth century five major centers of power had emerged on the Italian peninsula: the republics of Venice, Milan, and Florence; the Papal States; and the kingdom of Naples. Let's take a closer look at each of them.

Bell towers of San Gimignano

Major powers in Italy

Venice

Pleasantly situated on the Adriatic Sea in northeastern Italy, Venice had been a prosperous trading center for centuries. The city was built upon 118 small islands in a lagoon (a body of shallow water separated from the sea by sandbanks). Four hundred bridges linked the islands, which were, in turn, crisscrossed by small canals. Given Venice's coastal location and lack of good farming land, it is not surprising that its earliest settlers made their living from the sea.

Venice was made a republic in the eighth century. Ruled by a *Doge* (Duke) and a Great Council made up of 200 wealthy merchants, it gradually became the most highly organized government west of the Byzantine Empire. (Half of the members of the Great Council came from twenty-seven families!) The Doge had little actual power and mainly performed ceremonial duties. He was elected for life (by the Great Council) from among the noblest Venetian families and had to be of a "respectable age" (often at least seventy). It was the Senate, elected from the membership of the Great Council, that made the laws, while the *Collegeo* (the cabinet) directed foreign policy. A small group called the Council of Ten was elected annually to handle emergencies, such as declaring war, as they arose. Competition to wear the black robes of political office was keen. Those wealthy Venetians who failed to enter the Great Council by the age of twenty-five were referred to as *il trisi* (the sad ones).

Venetians were well aware that their prosperity depended upon their maritime trade. Beginning in 997, a lavish ceremony was celebrated annually on Ascension Day to acknowledge the city's gratitude to the sea. The state barge of the Doge, the Bucentaur, was decorated with gold and crimson cloth and towed into the Adriatic, followed by a procession of government leaders in gilded gondolas. When they reached the open sea, the Doge cast a golden ring into the waters, chanting, "Oh sea, we wed thee in sign of our true and everlasting dominion."

The Grand Canal in modern Venice

Although Venice was a republic, its citizens did not have a great deal of freedom. In fact, they were instructed by the Great Council to spy on their neighbors and to report any suspicious behavior. The open mouths of the masks that were carved onto the facades of government buildings served as slots into which citizens could drop their messages about suspected criminals. (The slots were called the "mouths of truth") There were no public trials. If the Council believed a person was guilty, he was strangled or left to slowly perish in a dungeon. Or he might be thrown in a special place in the lagoon where no fishing was allowed, or even buried upside down in the main piazza with his legs protruding above his grave! If an accusation was falsely made, the informer was simply fined.

The government carefully guarded the secrets of the city's main industry, glass-making. Venetian merchants had learned how to make glass from their contacts in the East, and the Council was determined to keep the knowledge from spreading to other European cities. Any workman in the glass industry who attempted to leave Venice was accused of treason, hunted down, and killed.

Saint Mark's Basilica, dedicated to the patron saint of Venice, was built in the eleventh century. It is a fine example of Byzantine architecture, with its large central dome and design of a Greek cross as well as the splendid mosaics that entirely cover its interior. Saint Mark's was first used as a private chapel by the Doge. Every Venetian merchant who traveled to the East was required by law to bring back some object for the cathedral.

In the thirteenth century an army of Christian Crusaders were diverted from their journey to Jerusalem by a sly old Doge named Enrico Dandolo. He offered to transport the soldiers and horses across the Mediterranean at bargain prices - if they would first attack Venice's rival trading city, Zara (on the eastern coast of the Adriatic Sea). The Crusaders agreed, overran the city of Zara and were dazzled by the rich spoils, to which they greedily helped themselves. This made it easy for Dandolo to convince them to attack the even richer city of Constantinople. The treasure-seeking Crusaders assaulted that ancient capital with tremendous fury, destroying buildings, killing innocent inhabitants, and stealing whatever treasures they found. A set of four bronze horses, looted from Constantinople, were placed over the porch of Saint Mark's Basilica in Venice. Today, they have been replaced by replicas, but you can see the original bronze horses inside Saint Mark's.

Saint Mark's Basilica

Milan Cathedral and an ancient Roman arch

a ruthless and ambitious tyrant, who achieved such clout on the European political scene that he was able to marry the daughter of King John II of France. (One of his sisters married a son of King Edward III of England.) To his credit, Visconti was also an early patron of the arts. The Milan Cathedral, the third largest church in Europe, was begun by his orders in 1385. Its huge roof is covered with 135 marble spires, each one bearing a religious statue. (The cathedral wasn't completed until Napoleon I oversaw its final stages in the early nineteenth century.) We'll learn more about the infamous Visconti family later in our story.

Francesco Sforza carried on his military tradition and became one of the greatest of the

With this gruesome episode, the monopoly of trade in the eastern Mediterranean passed from Constantinople to Venice. Genoa, in northwestern Italy, was a major trading rival until Venice conquered it in 1380. In the fifteenth century Venice reached the height of its powers. Venetians proudly referred to their city as *Serenissima* (the most serene).

Milan

The city of Milan was strategically sited on the Lombard plain along the main trade routes running from northern Italy through the alpine passes into Germany. Milan had been a center of trade in ancient times, and it regained this role as European commerce expanded in the eleventh century. It also grew famous for its manufacture of fine cloth and metal weapons.

Milan became a republic in the twelfth century, but beginning in the following century it was ruled by a series of despots. In 1395, Gian Galeazzo Visconti became duke of Milan. He was

The horses of Saint Mark's

The Papal Palace in Avignon, and the famous (half-built) Bridge of Avignon

condottieri. He married Bianca Maria Visconti, daughter of the last Visconti duke, and made himself Duke of Milan. His wife was as brave as he was. While he was away fighting a campaign, she led a band of soldiers to attack a rebellious town rather than send for her husband's help. With her at his side, Francesco made Milan one of the leading cities of the Italian Renaissance.

Their son, Galeazzo Maria Sforza, was taught by the finest humanists to be a perfect Renaissance prince. He learned to sing in French, to write in Latin, to read Greek, to play the organ and the clavichord, to dance, and to deliver lengthy classical speeches before the court. In 1466 he succeeded his father, and to everyone's surprise he told all humanists at court to leave, returned his Latin books to the library, and set about leading a life of debauchery. Three of his own courtiers murdered him a decade later.

The Papal States

The Papal States consisted of a wide band of territories in central Italy, which were ruled by the Pope. The heart of this region was the city of Rome. Once the magnificent capital when the mighty Roman Empire encompassed the Mediterranean Sea, Rome shrank to a town of only a few thousand inhabitants in the early Middle Ages. Several popes tried to revive the city as a monument to their authority, but the series of conflicts with the Holy Roman Emperors undermined their efforts, bringing bloodshed into its very streets. In 1309 things got so bad that the Pope was forced to flee to Avignon, France, leaving Rome to slide further into the abyss of squalor and despair.

The seat of the Papacy remained in Avignon for seventy years. This period is known as the Babylonian Captivity (a term derived from the time when the Jews were held captive in ancient Babylon). Freed from interference by the Pope, the Papal States were divided among the leading wealthy families and became independent kingdoms.

Pope Gregory XI returned to Rome in 1377, but France was not prepared to give up its control of the Papacy (all popes ruling from Avignon had been French). What followed was the Great Schism, when there was not one but two popes - one in Avignon and one in Rome! This division of power further weakened the Papacy. The conflict finally ended with election in 1417 of Martin V as the single Pope - with a residence in Rome.

The city Martin ruled was a mess! Visitors to Rome sadly described the once proud capital as a shadow of its former self, no better than a provincial town. No major construction had taken place there for years, and the old, decaying structures were either abandoned or shoddily patched up. Cattle grazed in the ancient forum (once the center of Rome's imperial government) while pigs rooted for tidbits wherever they could. No wonder someone referred to the city as a "rubbish heap of history." It was a slum. The violence in the streets was so bad that an organization called the "Brotherhood of Prayer and Death" made rounds at dawn to collect the bodies of men slain the night before! Martin did all he could to restore order, but as we will soon see, it was his successor, Nicholas V, who would take the first steps to make the city fit for a newer, grander Papacy.

The Kingdom of Naples

South of the Papal States was the Kingdom of Naples. In the late thirteenth century it was ruled not by an Italian but by Charles of Anjou, the brother of the French king. This region, although large in area, was relatively primitive. There were no major cities, apart from Naples, and most of the people were wheat farmers. The kingdom had once been united with the island of Sicily, which then fell into the hands of the Spanish. For centuries, this part of Italy was a battleground for French and Spanish aggressions and a launching site for attacks on the Papal States.

In 1486 King Ferrante of Naples put down an insurrection of his barons. What followed was a reign of terror, when Ferrante put to death each of his opponents, embalmed their bodies, and kept them on public view as a warning to others!

Florence

Florence was the birthplace of the Italian Renaissance, and as such it deserves our very close study. The city was founded in 59 BC on the ruins of an earlier Etruscan settlement by the legendary Roman general and statesman, Julius Caesar. Florence lies along the Arno River at the foot of the Apennine Mountains in the gently rolling hills of Tuscany. During the Middle Ages, the city began to prosper as merchants began importing wool from England and silk from the East for local workers to refine, dye, and weave into fine cloth. This would be the city's main industry for centuries to follow.

Early in the thirteenth century, the first craft guilds (called *arti*) were established in Florence. These were associations of merchants, artisans, and professionals (such as doctors and lawyers), formed to protect the rights of their members. Eventually there were twenty-one guilds. Each one had its own rules to control the quality of its product or service. Only the most skillful could join. Given the importance of the cloth industry in the Florentine economy, among the most important guilds were the *Arte della Lana* (the wool merchants), the *Arte di Camimala* (the cloth merchants), and the *Arte di Por* Santa Maria (the silk merchants). Equally prestigious was the Arte

The Arno River flows through Florence

della Seta, whose members wove and processed silk to create exquisite brocades, satins, and taffetas. Professional guilds included the *Arte del Cambio* (the bankers' guild) and the *Arte dei Medici, Speziali e Merciai* (the guild of doctors and apothecaries). Because of the materials they used, painters belonged to the same guild as the apothecaries. (Jars of colored pigment used for paint were to be found beside containers of herbs and other medicines in any apothecary shop.) Members of the major guilds looked down upon the minor ones, such as the guilds of butchers, vintners, tanners, and small-time tradesmen. In turn, these workers felt superior to the thousands of ordinary laborers - weavers, spinners, dyers, combers, carters, and others who did not belong to any guild at all. More than three-quarters of Florence's population fell into this last category.

By the end of the thirteenth century the guilds had gained control of the city government. As the merchants became the dominant class, the old families of the nobility lost much of their prestige and played a smaller role in Italian society than they had in earlier times. Some resourceful aristocrats used their talents to become businessmen, ambassadors to royal courts, or government officials.

The Florentine population was often torn apart by political factions. Remember the Guelfs and the Ghibellines? These two rival groups, which originally arose to support the interests of the Holy Roman Emperor (the Ghibellines) or the Pope (the Guelfs), continued to exist for generations. To advertise their allegiances, the Ghibellines wore white robes and white hats at political gatherings, and when they dined they cut their food sideways and drank out of goblets. The Guelfs, on the other hand, wore red robes and red hats, cut their food straight across, and drank wine out of cups! By the thirteenth century the Guelf party had recruited most of the merchant class of Florence and finally prevailed over the predominantly noble Ghibellines. (This is when Dante, a Ghibelline, was exiled from the city.)

The Guelfs then divided into rival parties of Black and White Guelfs, each of which competed for power in Florentine politics. The Whites felt uneasy about the Pope's political power and also worried about the interest France was taking in the Italian peninsula. They soon resembled the old Ghibelline faction. And so the Florentines continued to argue among themselves over the same basic issues.

The Palazzo Signoria

By the fourteenth century, the population of Florence had reached 100,000. The new stone and brick wall (with eleven gates) that was built in 1333 would contain the city and its citizens until the nineteenth century. Florence was now a republic whose political power extended throughout the surrounding region of Tuscany, encompassing six subject cities, including Pisa and Arezzo. The government was run by a city council (the *Signoria*). The council met in the Palazzo Signoria.

Every two months the names of guild members who were at least thirty years old were drawn from eight leather bags called *borse*. (The borse were always kept in the sacristy of the church of Santa Croce.) Men who were in debt were ineligible to serve on the council, as were those who had completed a recent term or who were closely related to men whose names had already been drawn.

The members of the council were known as Priori. There were never more than nine *Priori*, six of them representing the major guilds and three the minor ones. (Dante had been a Prior before his exile.) Like all northern Italians, the Florentines were extremely patriotic, and the council members took great pride in serving their government. For official functions, the Priori wore fine crimson coats with ermine lining, collars and cuffs. One of them was chosen to serve as *Gonfaloniere*, the standard bearer of the republic and custodian of the city's banner - a red lily on a white field. (The name "Florence" was supposedly derived from the lilies that grew along the banks of the Arno River.) The Gonfaloniere had gold stars embroidered on his coat to indicate his special status.

Lily, symbol of Florence

The Priori served short (two-month) terms in order to reduce the chances of corruption or favoritism. (This is strange reasoning, given the fact that the entire system catered to the interests of the "favored few.") In times of crisis, a public assembly (*parlamento*) was summoned, consisting of all male citizens over the age of fourteen. This assembly elected a small group to handle the crisis. The rest of the time the Priori dealt with local issues that arose. They received rather modest salaries, but during their terms of office they resided in the luxurious *Palazzo della Signoria*. There they were attended by a large staff of green-liveried servants, who met their every need and prepared excellent meals. Every evening they were entertained by a "buffoon" who told funny stories and sang comical songs.

The Florentine government was far from democratic. It excluded the aristocracy (the *Grandi* or "big men") as well as ordinary craftsmen and laborers (the Popolo Minuto or "little men"). In fact, most members of the old nobility had so little power that it became standard government procedure to ennoble a man who was making a nuisance of himself, thereby taking away his right to vote! The wealthy merchants made up a class known as the *Popolo Grasso* (fat men). They ran the show. The lowest class consisted of the unskilled workers. The only way they could show their dissatisfaction was by rioting, which they often did.

A City of Merchants

The prosperity that the cloth industry brought to Florence made the merchants receptive to the humanist ideal of carving out one's own destiny, financial or otherwise. So important was commercial success in Florence that to be rich was considered honorable, to be poor disgraced. A silk merchant named Gregorio Data stated it well: "A Florentine who is not a merchant, who has not traveled through the world, seeing foreign nations and peoples and then returned to Florence with some wealth, is a man who enjoys no esteem whatsoever."

The wealthy merchants often commissioned artists to paint walls or altarpieces in their local churches. One reason they did this was to atone for making a business profit. (This was considered sinful in the eyes of the Church. Remember how Giotto was commissioned to paint the frescoes in Padua by Enrico Scrovegni, who hoped to make up for his father's "sins" as a moneylender?) In later years, businessmen often kept a "conscience account" in which funds were set aside specifically for contributing to works of charity, just as their modern counterparts do. Of course, the merchants also savored their new status as benefactors. Like the citizens of ancient Rome, they were contributing to the well-being of their community.

In 1348 three galleys brought the Bubonic Plague to Genoa from the East. As we learned in the last chapter, the plague, known as the Black Death, rapidly spread throughout Europe. It killed over half of Florence's population. As death ravaged the cities of northern Italy, trade came to a near standstill, and the prices of all products dropped dramatically Those Italian merchants who survived the disease responded to the economic crisis in inventive ways. When the wool prices plummeted, many of them began importing more silk, while others turned to leather, furniture, and metal-work. Meanwhile, the low grain prices prompted Italian farmers to channel their efforts into the production of wine, olive oil, and cheese. These products have remained major factors in Italy's prosperity up to the present time.

The Republic Defies Tyranny

In the early fifteenth century (1402) the huge army of Gian Galleazo Visconti, Duke of Milan, advanced menacingly towards Florence. Visconti, who considered himself the heir of Julius Caesar, intended to bring all of northern Italy under his rule. Already he had subjugated the cities of Verona, Padua, Siena, Pisa, and Perugia. Florence, the only remaining obstacle to his ambitions, seemed isolated and extremely vulnerable. But its citizens were determined not to be beaten by the ruthless tyrant. They reinforced the city walls, armed themselves, and hoped for the best. Luck was on their side, and Visconti suddenly died. Florence had been spared, and soon afterwards Siena, Pisa, Perugia, and Bologna declared their independence of Milan.

The fact that they had stood so firmly in the face of tyranny filled the Florentines with tremendous pride. Remembering their classical heritage, they compared themselves to the early Romans, who defended their republic against all enemies. The glories of the ancient past took on a new meaning. Leonardo Bruni, a humanist scholar, wrote an ambitious twelve-volume work, The *History of the Florentine People* (the first major historical work of the Renaissance). Like Petrarch, Bruni felt a great kinship with the people of earlier times, and he once remarked, "I have the feeling that the days of Cicero and Demosthenes (a Greek orator) are much closer to me than the sixty years just past".

The Cities Unite

As we have learned, the rivalry among the Italian city-states was often intense. Sometimes the squabbles evolved into wars. Because the citizens themselves were reluctant to leave their businesses and join in the fighting, the governments began to hire professional soldiers. Soon most of the major city-states had armies of mercenary (hired) soldiers who were led by captains called *condottieri*. (The name "condottieri" comes from the contracts - *condotte* - that the captains signed to fight for a particular city for a certain length of time.) Sometimes the *condottieri* found themselves fighting against the very city that had paid them the previous month!

In 1454 a treaty known as the Peace of Lodi was signed by the five major powers of Italy - Venice, Milan, Florence, the Papal States, and the Kingdom of Naples. The Italians were spurred to take this measure by the recent conquest of Constantinople by the Ottoman Turks. (They worried, and rightly so, that the Turks might continue to gobble up parts of Europe.) But they also saw the commercial benefits of peace within Italy. According to the treaty's terms, each power was to recognize and respect the boundaries of the others. Should there be an attack by outsiders, the powers would unite for their mutual protection. Most important, they would stop squabbling with one another. The Peace of Lodi established a period of stability and prosperity in Italy that made it possible for all kinds of good things to happen.

Mantua

Apart from the major powers who signed the Peace of Lodi, there were a number of smaller city-states in Italy that contributed greatly to Renaissance culture. One of these was Mantua, near the Po River in northern Italy. It was surrounded by three artificial lakes. One of its major achievements was in education.

As we have seen, views of education had changed quite a bit since medieval times. In the early fifteenth century Pietro Paolo Vergerio

The skyline of Mantua

of Padua wrote a very important treatise on education, *On Noble Customs and Liberal Studies of Adolescents*. Vergerio advocated maintaining Latin as the core of liberal education, reviving the study of Greek, and pursuing a broad range of academic subjects as well as physical education. Using the ancient Greeks as his model, he proposed a return to the classical balance of body and spirit in a program that stressed athletics as well as scholarship. He believed that the goal of education was to bring out the best in every individual and to prepare children for a competitive life in the world of business.

Vergerio's treatise had a huge effect upon the ideas of Vittorino da Feltre, who is considered the greatest humanist schoolmaster of the Renaissance. He was invited by Gianfrancesco Gonzaga, Marquis of Mantua in 1423 to establish a school based on classical principles for his son and the sons of his principal courtiers. Classes met in the Duke's splendid villa, *La Casa Giocosa* (the Joyful House), whose walls were painted with bright pictures of children at play. In addition to the sons of prominent families, many poor children of ability were invited to attend, and all were treated on an equal basis.

Vittorino believed that learning should be fun (a novel concept in those times), and he was the first to use games to teach mathematics and movable letters to teach spelling. His students were

Vittorino da Feltre

not punished for working slowly (as they were in the traditional schools), but were simply required to finish their assignments while others played. Vittorino introduced his students to classical literature by reading aloud many of the Greek and Roman myths and legends. Later, the students read the ancient works on their own, carefully analyzing them and discussing the key ideas. The school also offered courses in swimming, horseback riding, and wrestling, as well as lessons in good manners. They students even went on field trips.

In later years, the number of students at La Giocosa grew to about seventy, many of whom boarded at the school. Even a few privileged girls attended, and poor boys of promising intellectual ability attended for free (they were among the first scholarship holders). Many students became important Italian rulers and professional men in many cities of Renaissance Italy.

Urbino

Among the students of the Joyful House was Federico da Montefeltro of Urbino. Urbino was a small duchy at the foothills of the northern Apennine Mountains. In 1444 Federico da Montefeltro became Urbino's new Duke when his elder brother died. He had been trained as a condottiere, and when he inherited Urbino he absorbed the surrounding mountain towns and made his duchy three times larger than it had been.

Federico was an able ruler, who divided his time between Urbino and the sites of his military ventures. As a condottiere he fought in the service of such powerful men as the dukes of Milan, the kings of Naples, and several popes. When he was home, he made a great effort to keep in touch with his subjects. He often went to the market, entering shops to exchange pleasantries and doffing his cap to everyone he met. This led to the common expression, to be "as busy as Federico's bonnet."

Thanks to having been educated by Vittorino da Feltre, Federico developed a lifelong love of books. He knew Greek and Latin well, and he enjoyed discussing topics as diverse as Julius Caesar's campaigns, Aristotle's philosophy, Livy's histories, and the writings of Saint Augustine.

Today Urbino looks much like it did during the Renaissance

Battista Sforza by Piero della Francesca

Federico da Montefeltro by Piero della Francesca

He hired five scholars to read aloud at dinner. One of his major goals, he once said, was to learn something new every day. Federico created the finest library since ancient times, which he prized above all his other possessions. He kept forty scribes busy for fourteen years copying manuscripts for his large collection. (The ducal library was later added to the Vatican Library.)

Federico used the wealth he earned as a condottiere to build an elegant palace, which he filled with beautiful statues and paintings. He attended Mass daily in his private chapel, but to show his love of the classics he had another chapel dedicated to the Greek muses built beside it. A true humanist, he saw no conflict between the ideals of the ancients and those of Christianity. In his study there were twenty-eight portraits of famous men, including the Greek poet Homer and the Roman playwright Seneca as well as Saint Thomas Aquinas and King Solomon.

The Duke's second wife was Battista Sforza, a member of the ruling dynasty in Milan. She married when she was only thirteen. Battista spoke Greek and Latin, was a patroness of the arts, and even governed Urbino when her husband was away. Together Federico and Battista presided over a glittering court that attracted humanists and artists from all over Europe. The 500 members of the court included 200 servants, four teachers, an astrologer, five "readers aloud at meals," forty transcribers of books, two organists, the keeper of the bloodhounds, and a man who tended the Duke's pet camel-leopard. Above are portraits of Federico and Battista painted by Tuscan artist Piero della Francesca in 1472.

Renaissance Women

You might think that well-off Renaissance women lived a charmed life, enjoying the poetry written in their honor by admiring courtiers or planning the new season's wardrobe. But even at the highest levels of society, women were not the equals of men. Not even close! In fact, those who smiled the sweetest and spoke the least were the most highly regarded by the court. The same was true among the lower classes, where women were expected to do as they were told by their fathers or husbands. It was a man's world, no doubt about that. Battista Sforza was, of course, an exception to this rule.

So what was the role of a woman? In most cases, her major duty was to have a baby every year. Children made up half the population in most European countries. (In those days, most people didn't live beyond the age of forty.) Families were very large in those early times because less than half of all children lived to adulthood. Magdalucia, the Venetian wife of a wealthy merchant, Francesco Marcello, gave birth to twenty-six children! (Thirteen survived to adulthood.) Sons were favored, in part because they continued the family name and, in the lower classes, because they could help out with the physical chores on the farm or in the workshop. The preference for male children can be seen in the records of babies abandoned at birth: the vast majority were girls.

Only the daughters of the wealthy received a formal education, and they generally learned only to converse well and play a musical instrument (and sing). They were taught at home, since respectable young ladies never left the house except to go to church. Only a handful of noblewomen actually read the classics. The majority of women remained illiterate. Their lives

were devoted to running the household, bearing and caring for the children, and making the family clothing.

A girl was expected to marry in her teens or to become a nun (if she was wealthy) or a servant (if she was poor). There were no other options. Marriage-bound daughters had to be provided with dowries (useful household materials as well as the ownership of property) in order to attract suitable husbands. A young maiden kept the linens of her dowry in a beautifully carved hope chest called a *cassone*, which was often passed down from mother to daughter. (Certain artists' workshops specialized in the production of the cassone.)

Marriages were arranged by parents for their own economic advantage, and love was seldom considered. (No sensible family would allow the acquisition of valuable property to be jeopardized by their daughter's lack of affection for her future spouse!) Since some middle class families could not afford dowries for all their daughters, the younger ones often ended up in convents against their wills. Imagine how terrible it must have been for a girl to be placed there if she had no religious calling. Actually, so many girls were forced to enter convents in sixteenth century Italy because they lacked suitable dowries (over twelve percent of the young women in Florence suffered this fate) that local communities began to establish special dowry funds. A sum of money was paid into the fund when a girl was born; at the age of fifteen she was repaid the sum with interest, and this provided her with a dowry.

Review Questions

1. What was the major industry in northern Italy?

2. What were the five major powers in Italy?

3. Who was the Doge and what were his duties?

4. What was the Babylonian Captivity?

5. Describe the Florentine craft guilds.

6. What was the Signoria?

7. How democratic was Florentine government?

8. Why did wealthy merchants often commission artists to paint the walls of churches?

9. What was a lucco?

10. What was a condottiere?

11. What was the Joyful House?

12. Describe the court of Federico da Montefeltro.

13. What was basic rule of a woman in fifteenth century Italy?

Further Thoughts

1. The core of Venetian naval power was its large fortress (the Arsenal) which contained shipyards and factories. This was the largest industrial complex of the Renaissance. (It was enclosed by two miles of fortifications.) It employed thousands of workers who used methods later seen in the modern assembly line. An early example of mass production, the Arsenal had ready made parts, such as oars, masts, and sails, and could build a complete galley in a very short time. Replacement parts were kept in ports all over the known world. The Venetian state leased the galleys to individual merchants, making a handsome profit.

The Arsenal in Venice

2. Even today Florence has a city council, which functions similarly to its fourteenth century model. (It meets, of course, in the Palazzo Vecchio, formerly the Palazzo della Signoria.) But the modern city has some problems never imagined in earlier times. Although its population numbers only 372,000, a relatively small number for a major city, Florence is invaded annually by nearly three million tourists who spend at least one night, and this doesn't account for day trippers! This means that there are seven tourists (overnight) per inhabitant!

3. Slaves were common in fifteenth century Florence. A well-to-do household had at least one. An owner had total power over his slaves, who

were treated as chattel and classified in inventories with domestic animals! Luckily, the children of slaves automatically became free citizens. Most slaves of fifteenth century Florence were Tartars captured in the region of the Black Sea. The government officially allowed the ownership of slaves provided they were not Christians!

4. Many processes were involved in changing the raw wool into cloth. Each was performed by a specialist. Spinners turned the wool to yard, dyers dyed it, weavers made it into cloth, fullers stepped the loose weave and pounded it firm, shear men raised the nap, cropped it, straightened and pressed the finished cloth.

5. Silk was first produced in China about 4,500 years ago. The silk threads come from the cocoon made by a silkworm for protection as it grows into a moth. To make silk fabric, the delicate threads of the cocoons are unwound and then twisted together into longer threads. These are woven on a loom to produce a beautiful and durable cloth. It takes over 2,500 cocoons to produce just twenty ounces of thread, which explains why silk is so expensive. For 2,000 years the process of making silk was a closely guarded secret.

6. To raise money to pay for shipping cargoes, Italian merchants sold shares in each venture to divide the costs and risks among several people. These joint stock companies were the forerunners of modern companies that sell stock to shareholders.

7. Elisabetta Gonzaga grew up in the court of Mantua and married the son of Federico and Battista. She brought to Urbino her own circle of scholars, artists, and musicians, making the court the most celebrated in Italy.

Projects

1. Each of the guilds of Florence had a special emblem painted on a shield. Consult the books in your classroom or library and find out what they were. Then, using poster board, draw five or six of them with colored markers. Be sure to label each one.

2. Draw a map of Italy, indicating the five major powers of the fourteenth and fifteenth centuries.

3. Draw a picture of a typical merchant and his wife of fifteenth century Florence.

4. Find out more about the condottieri. Who were some of the most famous captains? Write a short report.

5. Consult a book or find an article online about the Piazza della Signoria. Write a short history of the famous piazza, coming all the way up to modern times.

6. San Marino is an Italian city-state that has remained independent to the present day. Find out more about this interesting place and write a short report.

The Court of Mantua by Andrea Mantegna

CHAPTER 4

THE AGE OF THE MEDICI

Florentine art and architecture reached new heights in the fifteenth century when one family, the Medici, controlled the local government. During these rich years, the innovations of Giotto and the Pisani as well as the visions of the humanists were warmly embraced by new generations of artists and philosophers. Supported by the wealthy merchant class, an unusually talented group of men created the greatest works of the early Italian Renaissance.

Arrival of the Medici

The Medici first settled in Florence in the thirteenth century as cloth merchants. Their name suggests that their ancestors were pharmacists. (*Medici* means "preparers of medicine.") In later years, their enemies would mockingly refer to the clusters of red balls on the family crest as "those pills." The Medici were active in local politics, several members being appointed to the prestigious position of Gonfaloniere. There were also a few who were known as troublemakers. (Their names frequently appeared on lists of those sent into exile or involved in lawsuits.) But it was in banking that the family made its mark.

The Italian Bankers

Florence could never have had a thriving trade industry without solid financial backing. The Italians had long been considered the best bankers in Europe. They were always present at the major trading centers in France and Germany to exchange one currency for another, making a good profit in the process. In fact, the word "bank"

comes from the *banco* (bench) the money changers sat upon. They also issued bills of exchange - letters written by bankers in one country instructing those in another to make payments in the local currency to the bearers of the bills. It was even an Italian - a Franciscan monk named Fra Luca Pacioli - who created the double entry system of accounting to record the assets and liabilities of a company.

Several Italian families, such as the Bardi and the Peruzzi of Florence, used the money they had amassed in the cloth industry to create their own large banking houses. They handled such huge sums that kings and emperors often came to them when they needed funds to pay their armies, to build new palaces, or simply to cover bribes. This made the families even wealthier and tremendously influential. Often, the banking houses had branches in more than one city. The major financial street in modern London is Lombard Street, which was named after the Italian moneylenders from Lombardy who settled there in the thirteenth century.

A gold florin issued in 1256

Florence soon became the banking center of Europe. The city's currency, the gold florin, was first minted in 1252. It contained exactly 3.5 grams of gold, and this amount remained unchanged until 1533, making the florin the most stable currency of its day. One side of the coin was stamped with the city's Latin name, *Florentia*, and a portrait of John the Baptist, the city's patron saint. On the obverse side appeared the lily, the symbol of Florence. In time, the florin became the international currency of western Europe, overtaking the Venetian ducat. In 1420 there were 2,000,000 florins in circulation (and seventy-two bankers in the city of Florence).

The Establishment of the Medici Bank

Giovanni di Bicci de Medici (1360-1429) used his wife's dowry to found a bank. By investing in trading companies (in which he demanded a controlling interest) and obtaining a monopoly of the finances of the Pope (a truly major client), Giovanni made his bank the biggest in Florence. His personal wealth of 80,000 florins could have paid the annual salaries of 2,000 laborers in the cloth industry. To ease his conscience for being a "sinful banker" (remember how the Church condemned making a profit through business?), Giovanni spent much of his wealth on the construction of churches, the support of art, and contributions to charity. These activities helped to conceal his genuine love of money behind the facade of philanthropy and concern for the public good. We will soon see how his descendants followed his lead in patronizing the arts to glorify the family image. Giovanni served several terms in the Signoria, and in 1421 he was chosen Gonfaloniere.

Cosimo de Medici

Cosimo de Medici (1389-1464), the son of Giovanni, was a financial genius. He helped his father make the Medici bank one of the most profitable businesses in Europe. Thanks to his efforts, the bank had branches in sixteen major cities. When Cosimo was nearly forty, Giovanni died, leaving his son his immense financial wealth and political clout. Soon afterwards, Cosimo challenged the power of the ruling family of Florence, the Abrizzi. They temporarily stopped him in his tracks by arranging for his arrest (he was accused of fraud). Cosimo was held in a cramped cell in the bell tower of the Palazzo della Signoria. But the Abrizzi hadn't recognized the extent of Medici influence. In reward for his generosity in the past, one of the conspirators set Cosimo free, and he fled the city. He was warmly welcomed everywhere - the Venetians even staged his triumphal entrance into their city. Meanwhile, the Florentine economy began to flounder, so Cosimo was summoned home. Now it was the Abrizzi who were sent into exile, while Cosimo set about consolidating his control of the city. In time he would become in fact, if not in name, the unchallenged ruler of Florence.

As a young man Cosimo had studied the writings of the ancients, and he had been impressed by the Greek ideal of moderation in one's life. ("Nothing in excess" was a well-known Greek motto.) He applied this principle to his business dealings, always proceeding in a prudent and cautious manner. He occasionally took risks, but only when the odds for success were extremely good. He was a practical man who enjoyed solving problems by skillful negotiation. Cosimo once remarked, "You may pursue the infinite, but I pursue the finite; you may set your ladder against the vaulted heavens, but I set mine firmly on the ground."

Determined not to flaunt his great wealth, Cosimo took great care to appear as an ordinary citizen, drinking local wine, dressing modestly, and riding a mule rather than a horse. He was publicly genial and approachable, greeting hundreds of fellow citizens by name. He was also an uncanny judge of character.

Unlike his father, Cosimo had political ambitions that went beyond the role of Gonfaloniere. By using his family funds to bribe citizens to vote into power the men he favored, he managed to govern Florence for thirty years without ever receiving an official title. The Medici bank furnished or denied loans to the Florentine government according to how Cosimo felt about the current political situation. Most people willingly supported his views, reasoning that what was good for the Medici bank was good for Florence.

The Medici Palace

Cosimo commissioned the highly esteemed architect, Michelozzo, to design a town palace (*palazzo*) to serve as his family residence. It was built at the corner of Via Largo, the widest street in Florence at that time. Cosimo chose a simple, austere design and an unimposing outer surface of rusticated (unfinished) stone. Its four three-story wings formed a square around a courtyard. The building included business offices and storerooms on the ground floor. Despite the practical reasons for the palazzo's large dimensions, Cosimo's critics were quick to complain that he had built a palace that would

"throw even the Colosseum at Rome into the shade." However, it became the model for all noble

Interior of Medici Palace

Florentine houses built after it in the fifteenth century.

In 1439 Cosimo arranged for Florence to host the ecumenical council, which had been working vainly for years to reconcile the Roman Catholic and Eastern Orthodox Churches. The Pope, the Patriarch of Constantinople, and the Holy Roman Emperor were his personal guests at the newly completed palazzo. Cosimo saw to it that these celebrities were lavishly entertained with spectacular processions and festive banquets. It seemed as though Florence had become the most important place on earth, which, of course, was one of the banker's primary goals.

Cosimo used his diplomatic skills to end the long feud between Florence and Milan with the signing of the Peace of Cavriana 1441. Nine years later, he financed Francesco Sforza, an ambitious condottiere, in his successful effort to overthrow the Visconti dynasty that had ruled Milan for generations. Medici loans kept Sforza's new government afloat and made the former soldier a strong and grateful ally. The bank even served as a buffer against invasion. When Venice and the Kingdom of Naples joined forces against Florence, Cosimo recalled loans he had previously made to them and paralyzed their military operations! He later played an important role in the creation of the Italian League, formed by the five major powers of Italy after the Peace of Lodi.

Despite his efforts to seem like "one of the people," Cosimo was, in fact, the first of the "merchant princes" of Florence. He presided over a court that included the most celebrated Italian artists and scholars of the day. Believing that artists were people of extraordinary talent, who should be treated like celestial spirits, not beasts of burden, he paid them well for their efforts. In fact, he became the most generous and discriminating art patron Florence had ever known. He had a lot

to do with the changing image of the artist from manual laborer to creative genius.

Cosimo was well versed in Latin, and he adored books and manuscripts. He encouraged his friends to take an interest in learning by allowing them to borrow from his vast library. He loaned money to impoverished students and even founded the Platonic Academy, which became a center for the discussion of humanist ideas. Marsilio Ficino was the leading member of the Academy. His edition of the works of Plato (the first complete translation of Plato into Latin) made the Greek philosopher's ideas readily available to western scholars. Ficino believed that classical philosophy and the Christian religion were in harmony with one other, and he played a major part in bringing the pagan themes of the ancient world into Christian art.

The Medici Palace contained a large private chapel. In 1559 Cosimo hired Benozzo Gozzoli, a skilled artist, to paint frescoes on three of the walls depicting the Procession of the Magi (the three wise men who took gifts to the Christ child). Actually, the true purpose of the cycle of paintings was to depict the important people who had attended the Council of Florence twenty years earlier. Cosimo was still feeling proud of having hosted the meetings.

On the first wall, the youngest king leads the procession. He is said to represent Lorenzo, the grandson of Cosimo, although he was just a boy at the time. Behind him ride Cosimo himself, on a mule, and his son, Piero, on a prancing white horse. On the second wall is the second king, who has the facial features of the Byzantine emperor. On the third wall the oldest king is none other than the Patriarch of Constantinople. Following along on foot in the paintings are a number of important Florentines, such as philosopher Marsilio Ficino. The artist even included himself.

The Youngest King in the Procession of the Magi

Although the event of the birth of Christ took place in the Middle East, Gozzoli's figures are proceeding through a Tuscan landscape. And the people are dressed in the latest Florentine fashion.

Cosimo spent 40,000 florins renovating the convent of San Marco, including a library to house classical texts. The new structure was designed by the highly respected architect of the times, Michelozzo. Cosimo hired an artist, a Dominican friar known as Fra (Brother) Angelico, to paint the various rooms of the monastery with frescoes depicting scenes from the life of Jesus. Fra Angelico admired the works of Masaccio and understood the rules of linear perspective. He produced some of the most beautiful yet simple paintings of the period in Florence. Fra Angelico painted *The Annunciation* in one of the monks' cells (small

bedrooms) in the monastery. It depicts that key moment in the Christian story when the angel Gabriel appears to Mary, announcing that she will give birth to a son (Jesus) by miraculous means. The monk who slept in this cell would spend many hours praying in front of the friar's beautiful fresco. The scene seems to be taking place right there in San Marco – you can see an open doorway behind Mary (the figure there is Saint Dominic) and a small window of the kind that you can still see in the monks' cells in this bedroom.

Cosimo reserved a two-room cell for himself at San Marco so he might rest, read, meditate, and be reminded of the simpler aspects of life. He had been strongly encouraged to do this by the Pope, who told him he needed to demonstrate his religious devotion to balance (or perhaps to

The Annunciation by Fra Angelico

Cloister of San Marco

atone for) the great riches he was accumulating as the monopoly banker of the Church. Cosimo also oversaw the construction the church of San Lorenzo, which would later house his library.

In 1464 Cosimo died peacefully in extreme old age while listening to a reading of Ficino's translation of Plato. For several weeks before his death he often sat alone in a chair with his eyes closed. When asked why he did this, he responded, "to get used to the dark." He was posthumously given the title *Pater Patriae* (Father of the Nation) by his native city. This prestigious title had been awarded in the past to the mightiest emperor of Rome, Augustus. It was inscribed on Cosimo's tombstone in the crypt at San Lorenzo.

Florentine Fashions

Gozzoli's painting of the Procession of the Magi gives us a good idea of how very wealthy Florentines dressed. The basic attire of a merchant or craftsman was a loose fitting, long-sleeved shirt and long wool stockings, which were fastened with ties to the shirt. Late in the fifteenth century, the stockings came up to the waist - in fact, they were similar to our modern tights. Over his long shirt an older man, or someone of an important social status, would wear a *lucco* -an ankle-length gown of black or dark purple cloth with long wide sleeves, a

A fashionable young man from a 15th century mural by Domenico Ghirlandaio

hood, and buttons (a recent invention) down the front. A well-off younger man would wear a shorter sleeveless tunic rather than a lucco.

Footwear generally consisted of sheepskin or chamois boots. In the late fourteenth century, fashionable men wore very pointed shoes called poulaines. Sometimes the toes were stuffed with rags to exaggerate their length, which sometimes measured six inches or more. Eventually, the points went out of style and round toes were in. But then, in the 1460's, pointed shoes became all the rage again. This time the toes got so long they had to be chained and fastened at the knees!

A man wearing poulaines

Most men had their hair cut about shoulder length, and they used curling tongs to make it turn under. They wore a wide variety of hats, the most popular style being the *mazzocchino* (a woolen cloth rolled into a crown with the free end

drooping over the shoulder). Some young dandies wore a round felt hat called a *cupolina tondo* (little round dome). Italian men of the humbler classes - laborers and peasants - wore shirts and trousers made from coarse woolen cloth. Not so concerned with the latest fashion, they were probably more comfortable than their wealthier neighbors.

The typical Italian merchant's wife was renowned for her elegant and sumptuous clothes, which were primarily intended to show off her husband's commercial success. Her undergarment was a chemise, a long version of a man's shirt which fell to her ankles. Over this she wore a simple, flowing dress with a tight bodice and a high neckline. Next came a brightly colored silk or brocade overdress heavily embroidered with flowers, fruits and scrolls, gold thread, pearls, or other jewels. On her feet she wore soft leather slippers. The wardrobe of a merchant's wife might

Florentine men's fashions

Florentine womens' fashions

cost more than the house she lived in! The women of the lower classes made their dresses from plain woolen cloth, which they sometimes embroidered.

Since the fashion demanded a pale skin and fair hair, wealthy Florentine women, who tended to be dark haired and olive skinned, dyed their hair (or wore a wig of white or yellow silk) and bleached or powdered their skin. They wore many kinds of elaborate head dresses, such as the high, cone-shaped hennin, which rose three to four feet high and was draped with a veil. Compared to modern times, the people of the fifteenth century had few articles of clothing. Even the wealthy owned only a few outfits. Children wore clothing made from the castoffs of the adults. They never knew the luxury of jeans and sweatshirts but were condemned to wear uncomfortable miniature versions of their parents' costumes. A well-to-do family would often distribute fashionable clothing to all of their servants so that the entire household would favorably impress a visitor.

There were no dry cleaners in those days. A housewife (or her servants) boiled the linens and scrubbed the wools with homemade lye soap. Grease spots were rubbed with fuller's earth (an absorbent, clay-like substance moistened with lye). Silks were gently washed in heated water. When brocades, gold or silver tissues were badly worn, they were burned to recover the valuable metals.

Although bathing soap was invented in England in the fourteenth century, it did not become an important household item in Europe for a long time. The well-to-do took a bath every few weeks (less often in the winter), and the rest of the time they relied heavily on perfume to cover up any foul body odors. Many people carried perfumed handkerchiefs or wore small perfume bottles as pendants on necklaces.

A Stellar Trio

Good things often come in threes. Fifteenth century Florence produced a trio of artistic geniuses - Donatello, Brunelleschi, and Masaccio. They were the brightest stars of the Medici court. Like Giotto and the Pisani, they were inspired by the masters of antiquity. Their extraordinary works mark the beginning of the Italian Renaissance. (Giotto and the Pisani are considered forerunners of the age.)

Marzocco

Donatello

Donatello (Donato di Bette Bardi, 1386-1466) was a gifted sculptor. Like Giotto, he sketched the people of Florence as they went about their daily activities, and he used a live model whenever he sculpted. So committed was he to creating realistic works of art that he was once heard to exclaim to a statue he was sculpting, "Speak then! Why will you not speak?" Indeed, many of his figures appear to be frozen in a dramatic moment in time, and this theatrical element helps them to "come alive" for anyone who views them.

The young sculptor established his reputation with his marble statue of Saint George (the legendary dragon slayer). This work, which originally stood in the niche of a guild building, was the first Renaissance statue to stand unsupported against a wall (unlike the traditional relief statues).

In 1420 Donatello sculpted Marzocco, a heraldic lion that became a symbol of Florence. It was placed atop a column by the papal apartments of Santa Maria Novella. (Pope Martin V stayed there when he had just been elected pope.) Holding a shield emblazoned with the Florentine emblem, the *fleur de lis* (lily), Marzocco symbolized the city's strength and independence. His name is derived from *Martocus* (little Mars). The Roman god of war (Mars) was the patron deity of ancient Florence. The statue was moved to the Piazza della Signoria in 1812.

Donatello's greatest work was of *David*, a bronze statue of the biblical hero commissioned by the city of Florence and completed in 1430. Bronze was a popular medium in ancient times, but medieval statues were usually carved in stone or wood. Donatello's *David* was the first life-size bronze free-standing statue since antiquity (and also the first nude). David stands in the classical pose of *contrapposto* (a relaxed position in which his weight is placed on one foot and his opposing shoulder is raised). Imagine yourself waiting for something in a long line of people. Wouldn't you be standing in this position, rather than with your weight equally distributed on both feet? The ancient sculptors often used the

David

contrapposto pose to make their statues appear natural, but the technique had been forgotten for centuries until Donatello rediscovered it. David gazes down on the head of the slain Goliath. He embodies youthful grace and dignity; his nudity (a symbol of his vulnerability) is emphasized by the hat and greaves (leg armor) he wears.

Gattemelata

The statue became a symbol of Florentine liberty. (The winged helmet worn by Goliath was a symbol of Milan's Visconti family. Remember how Florence had stood tall against Milan?) It was originally placed in the courtyard of the palace of Cosimo de Medici, mounted on a base engraved with an inscription extolling Florentine heroism and virtue.

According to legend, Cosimo was so impressed by Donatello's talents that he gave him a stylish new wardrobe. However, the young sculptor was too embarrassed to wear such fine clothes, and so he returned them. (Fifty years later, artists would dress like courtiers, as we will see. But the time had not yet come.) This is not to say that Donatello did not take tremendous pride in his work. He once furiously broke a head that he had sculpted because the merchant who ordered it offered him too low a price!

In 1445 Donatello began his huge bronze equestrian statue of the renowned condottiere Erasmo da Narni - nicknamed Il Gattemelata ("the Slick Cat"). It was modeled after the sole surviving ancient Roman equestrian statue, that of Emperor Marcus Aurelius. (The Roman statue had escaped destruction by anti-pagan zealots in the late years of the Empire because it was wrongly believed to represent Christian Emperor Constantine!) This time Donatello "reinvented" the ancient technique of portraying a great general on horseback. The "Slick Cat" sits proudly in the saddle, a model of commanding energy.

Mary Magdalene

The late works of Donatello reflect more violent emotions than his earlier statues. A good example is his wooden sculpture of Mary Magdelen, who was reputed to be a sinful woman. According to tradition, Mary Magdelen used her ill-gotten fortune to help Christ and became his only female friend. After he was crucified, she took refuge in a cave in France where, for thirty years, she atoned for her earlier sins. While artists traditionally depicted her as young and beautiful, Donatello's figure is an emaciated, vacant-eyed old woman dressed in animal skins - a vivid portrayal of the ravages of aging and the horrible effects caused by years of self-denial.

Donatello's statues were famous in his own time, and generations of sculptors would take their cues from his innovations before setting out to give form to their own artistic visions. When he died in 1466, the artist's body was placed in a tomb near that of Cosimo de Medici in the Florentine church of San Lorenzo.

Statue of Brunelleschi

committee in charge chose the more traditionally arranged figures of Ghiberti by a narrow margin.

The Gates of Paradise

Brunelleschi

Filippo Brunelleschi (1377-1446) is known as an architect, but he was originally trained as a goldsmith and sculptor. In 1401 he entered a competition sponsored by the Guild of Cloth Importers (the Arte di Calimala) to design a set of doors of the Florence Baptistery. (The Baptistery was situated near the Cathedral and, as its name implies, was used for baptism.) The seven greatest sculptors of the day were pitted against one another. They were asked to create a bronze relief sculpture depicting the biblical story of the sacrifice of Isaac. The finalists were Brunelleschi and Lorenzo Ghiberti, and after much debate the

Ghiberti would spend the next twenty-five years creating beautiful bronze panels for the doors illustrating many episodes from the Old Testament. When at last they were completed, Ghiberti was immediately commissioned by the guild to produce a second set. These ten panels, each one depicting several different episodes from the Bible, became the sculptor's masterpiece. When the panels were revealed to the public, the acclaim was unprecedented. The figures are so realistic and emotionally inspiring that the artist Michelangelo later remarked that the doors could grace the gates to Paradise. (They've been known as the Gates of Paradise ever since.) Ghiberti had good reason to be proud of his accomplishments, and he decided to write an autobiography (entitled *Commentari*). He was the first artist to write a book about himself. However, he stretched the truth somewhat when he wrote, "Few things of importance have been done in our land where I have not had a hand in the design or the direction." He was even more arrogant than Giovanni Pisano!

But let's return to Brunelleschi. He was so disappointed by his failure to win the competition that he gave up sculpture completely and turned to architecture. This seems like an abrupt change of direction, but, as we'll soon see, artists of this period often tried their skills at more than one discipline. Brunelleschi's decision turned out to be a good thing, too, since he became the greatest architect of the early Italian Renaissance.

About this time, he became friendly with the young Donatello, and the two decided to travel together to Rome. There the budding architect analyzed and measured the ancient ruins and drew sketches of them, while Donatello carefully studied the statues. Brunelleschi was impressed by the simple, balanced lines of the Roman buildings: their rounded arches, straight columns and domed roofs seemed to blend perfectly together to form a symmetrical unit. The two young artists became so enraptured with the ancient works that they decided to base all their future creative enterprises on those of antiquity. They were soon referring to themselves as "the heirs of Rome," although other artists, noting the collection of ancient coins and gems they had amassed, dismissed them as "treasure seekers."

In 1418 the Guild of Wool Merchants in Florence announced a competition to design a dome for the Cathedral of Santa Maria del Fiore (known as the Duomo). This Gothic building had been started in 1294 but was not completed. The original architect (Arnolfo di Cambio) had been instructed to design a church "so magnificent in size and beauty as to surpass anything built by the Greeks and Romans." Arnolfo obliged by building the world's largest Catholic church. (Today it is surpassed only by Saint Peter's in Rome, Saint Paul's in London, and the Cathedral in Milan.) Unfortunately, Arnolfo died before figuring out how to cover the enormous octagonal opening, which required a domed roof larger than any built before.

Interior of the dome of the Pantheon

Brunelleschi thought about the domed structures he had seen in Rome, particularly the Pantheon. Then he consulted the ten books on architecture written by Roman engineer Pollio Vitruvius (the only treatise on architecture that had survived from the ancient world). Pouring over these volumes of the past and pondering the sketches he had made in Rome, he slowly came up with a revolutionary design for the dome.

The huge size was the greatest challenge. Normally a builder would use a temporary wooden framework shaped like a hemisphere to support the construction of the dome until the mortar had hardened. However, the base of the cathedral's dome was more than 136 feet in diameter, and no trees could be found to span so wide a space. Even if the wood was available, the framework would have collapsed under its own weight. Someone suggested that the space beneath the proposed dome be filled with earth containing random handfuls of coins to support the construction. When the dome was completed, the children of Florence could dash in, dig for the coins, and take away the earth at the same time!

Brunelleschi had a better idea. He designed a double dome with a strong inner shell that would support most of the weight and a light outer one. He would build the inner dome one layer of bricks at a time, the weight of each new layer supported by the one previously constructed. Each row would be stepped slightly inward, creating a herringbone pattern, so as the construction proceeded the structure would gradually taper toward the center. For added strength, a masonry of eight massive self-supporting stone ribs would be built. With this plan, no wooden framework or scaffolding would be needed inside the dome.

Between this inner shell and the outer one would be a complex web of smaller ribs and connecting horizontal buttresses that would tie the principal ribs together. A stairway between the shells would be used instead of scaffolding for the workers. (It is still possible to walk there.) Crowning the top there would be a lantern (a small structure admitting light into the interior). The dome would be elegant in its simplicity, majestic in its size.

Brunelleschi nearly did not get the job because he refused to show anyone his plans before he started work. He explained that if the other architects saw his model, they would steal his ideas. When the guild committee members remained adamant in their demands to see his design, he challenged them to stand an egg on its end. No one could, so Brunelleschi banged the egg on the table and stood it on its cracked top. When the committee complained that anyone could do that, the architect replied, "Yes, and you would say the same thing if I told you how to build the dome!" They allowed him to go ahead, but his old rival, Lorenzo Ghiberti, was appointed to help him (and keep an eye on him). Furious and insulted, Brunelleschi protested so loudly about Ghiberti's inexperience in architectural design that the committee reluctantly gave in and let him work alone. This must have really embarrassed the arrogant Ghiberti!

Brunelleschi's dome

Work began on the dome in 1421. Brunelleschi gathered such a vast supply of bricks, marble tiles, timbers, and stones that it seemed like he was building a dome over the entire city. As the project progressed, he ingeniously solved the smaller problems that arose. He invented a hoisting machine with pulleys so that the masons wouldn't have to carry up their materials. He designed guttering to drain off rain water and small openings to provide light and reduce wind force. He installed mini-restaurants in the work area so that the laborers didn't have to descend for their meals. He even inserted hooks to hold up scaffolding for future cleaning or repairs. And he consistently praised the efforts of the hardworking men. People who stopped by to observe the construction were astonished to see that the structure was indeed taking shape with no visible scaffolding or supporting framework.

Skyline of Florence

It took sixteen years to build the dome. Actually, it was completed after Brunelleschi's death by a younger architect, Michelozzo (the same man who designed Cosimo's palazza). Rising over 300 above the ground and vaulting a wider space than had ever been spanned before, the dome was an amazing achievement - a triumph of human genius and ingenuity. Although linked to medieval design in its use of ribs, its simplicity and symmetry recalled the best of the classical past. The Duomo became a model for all future domed buildings, and even today it is the focal point of Florence's skyline.

When plans for the dome were still on the drawing board, Brunelleschi began work on the Osperdale degli Innocenti (Foundling Hospital) in Florence. He loved the geometric designs involved in classical architecture - the circles and squares, hemispheres and cubes that combine to create a unified whole. He was particularly drawn to the form of the rounded arch, which he incorporated into a colonnade (a series of wide arches separated by slender columns) for the facade of the Hospital. With mathematical precision the height of each column equals the width of the bay between columns and also its depth from column to wall. As a result, each bay is really a cube of space. By combining the classical columns, arches, and pilasters (column-like structures attached to the wall) and stressing their geometric lines Brunelleschi defined the new Renaissance style of architecture.

He managed to find time to work on several other buildings, including the Florentine churches of Santa Maria degli Angeli, San Lorenzo, and Santo Spirito as well as the elegant Pazzi Chapel in Santa Croce. Each new building was a refinement of his geometric style. Every column, arch and pilaster was designed in direct proportion to the other elements, the many integral features forming a harmonious unit. Times were certainly changing. The pointed arches and soaring vaults of the medieval Gothic churches that reached towards the heavens were gradually being replaced by structures that seemed to hug the earth.

Osperdale degli Innocenti

Renaissance architecture reflects, in stone and bricks, spirit of humanism.

Around 1420 Brunelleschi painted two panels to demonstrate his theory of linear perspective. (Linear perspective refers to creating a sense of depth or receding distance on a flat surface). His ideas were probably derived from his careful studies of architectural design. According to his theory, all parallel lines in the foreground of a painting should converge at a single vanishing point on the horizon. (Imagine yourself standing on a huge lawn that has just been mowed. Look at the far end of the lawn. Don't the lines made by the lawn mower seem to come together in the distance?) Brunelleschi pointed out that close-up figures should appear larger than distant ones. (This seems obvious to us now, but back then most artists continued to follow the medieval formula of basing the size of a subject on his importance.) Brunelleschi's theory of perspective certainly makes sense, and it would strongly influence the painters who lived after him.

Cosimo de Medici had such great respect for the talented artists he patronized that he referred to them as "celestial spirits." Brunelleschi agreed with that judgment, adding that painting, sculpture, and architecture were not mechanical arts (like carpentry) but liberal ones (like mathematics and poetry). A picture, statue, or building was as much a product of the mind as of the hand; the true artist was not a mere craftsman but a man of learning and imagination.

By his achievements and by his words, Brunelleschi set the groundwork for a whole new definition of architecture and art. Sadly, he never saw the completion of any of his major structures. Like an omen from the Olympian gods, a lightning bolt struck (but did not

The Pazzi Chapel

damage) his uncompleted dome just a few months before he died.

Masaccio

The third in the trio of great artists was Masaccio (Tommaso di Giovanni di Simone Guidi, 1401-1428). He was nicknamed *Masaccio* ("Slovenly Tom") because he was so involved in his artistic endeavors that he paid little attention to his personal appearance. A friend of Donatello and Brunelleschi, he is considered the greatest painter of the early Italian Renaissance.

Masaccio greatly admired the works of Giotto and set out to emulate them. He studied human anatomy so that his figures would be lifelike. He experimented with the interplay of light and darkness, painting shadows so as to give definition to the forms they fell across. This technique is known as *chiaroscuro*, from the Italian words chiaro (bright) and *oscuro* (dark). It produces the illusion of roundness and weight in an object or figure. In many of Masaccio's works the light comes from a single source or direction. In addition, his broad, quick brush strokes suggest motion and drama.

Masaccio became the first artist to use Brunelleschi's principles of linear perspective in a major painting when he produced his fresco of the Holy Trinity in the church of Santa Maria Novella in Florence. He created the illusion of a chapel receding into the wall on which it is painted, and he reinforced the effect by placing the figures on a shelf that seems to project forward. The picture is composed in such a way that our attention is drawn toward the focal point of the work, a pyramidal group composed of the Virgin and Saint John at the bases and God the Father and the crucified Christ at the apex. Massacio's fresco marks the beginning of a new method of arrangement of figures based upon geometric forms. We'll see this again and again.

Holy Trinity

The Tribute Money

His greatest works are the frescoes he painted in the chapel of the Brancacci family in the church of Santa Maria del Carmine, Florence. The scene of *The Expulsion of Adam and Eve* is an intense psychological drama. The naked forms of the grief-stricken couple are molded in light and shadow, which gives them form and substance as they tearfully stride out of Paradise.

Another fresco, entitled *The Tribute Money*, depicts the Apostles gathered in a circle around Christ as they are confronted by a tax collector. Again, light and shadow give each figure a solid appearance. Christ's instruction to Peter to pay the tax collector is told through solemn gestures and expressions. According to the Bible, when the tax man came to collect tribute, Christ told Peter he could find the money in the mouth of a fish in the nearby Sea of Galilee. Peter cast for the fish, found the coin, and paid the man. In the fresco, Peter appears in the distance to the left, finding the coin. (It has been proposed that this picture symbolizes the Florentines' despair at having to pay an extra tax to support the fight against Milan.) By arranging the figures of this simple scene in a semicircle around Christ, the artist adapted the circle Brunelleschi employed in architecture.

Masaccio amazed his contemporaries with the dramatic and lifelike quality of his paintings. By the late fifteenth century, the Brancacci Chapel became a major point of pilgrimage for nearly every Italian artist. Sadly, Masaccio died at the age of twenty-seven. Imagine the great art he would have left to us had he lived longer.

So there we have the incredibly talented trio of Donatello, Brunelleschi, and Masaccio - sculptor, architect, and painter - who broke the boundaries of convention, merging their own innovative techniques with traditions of the past. Thanks to them, art was rapidly evolving from the medieval style of humanized faith into a lifelike representation of mankind. The Italian Renaissance was in full swing!

The Treatises of Alberti

In 1435 humanist and architect Leon Battista Alberti wrote a treatise explaining Brunelleschi's theories about perspective in a book entitled On Painting. The Italian translation was dedicated to Brunelleschi himself, the original having been written in Latin. Alberti considered art a branch of science, and his book explains how the artist

Santa Maria Novella

should employ principles of mathematics and geometry to depict the physical world.

Alberti's ten volumes on architecture (*On the Art of Building*) represent the first major treatise on that subject since the one by the Roman Vitruvius, on which it was loosely modeled. Alberti defined architecture as a noble science and the architect as a well-educated man of genius who applies his talents masterfully. Like Brunelleschi, he loved the simplicity and symmetry of classical design, which, he believed, reflect the order and balance of the natural world.

Alberti's writings played a central role in spreading the new theories of art and architecture. Conversations between artists now centered upon vanishing points, lines, and angles, and the subjects of their works were described in terms of squares and cubes. Some people really got carried away and emphasized perspective over content -in many of these, arch after arch recede into the vanishing point in the distance. Paolo Uccello (1397-1475) became so enamored with the new techniques that one night his wife found he

muttering again and again, "What a wonderful thing is perspective!"

Alberti designed many buildings in Florence, Rimini, and Mantua. His black and white marble main facade of the church of Santa Maria Novella in Florence is a fine example of geometric design and classical proportions. It fits into a perfect square, and a second square within the large square, encompassing the upper story and pediment, has an area exactly half that of the main section.

In addition to his work in art and architecture, Alberti wrote about sculpture, moral philosophy, marriage, horses, agriculture, Roman ruins, secret codes, applied mathematics, law, music, and the Tuscan dialect, among other things. He was also a poet, a social commentator, and an adviser in half a dozen princely courts in Italy. He even wrote and passed off as genuine a comedy attributed to a Roman playwright. And he was a gymnast who could leap over a man's head with his feet tied together! Alberti exemplified his own belief that "men can do all things" and is a shining example of a new ideal of his age, the multi-talented "Renaissance man."

A Booming City

By the middle of the fifteenth century, Florence had become one of the largest cities in Europe. Brunelleschi's dome hailed the city's renown as a center of art and culture. In fact, "Dome-sickness" was the term used to describe the sadness (home-sickness) that afflicted Florentines when they traveled to other places.

It was a boom period. Trade and business had never been better, and rich merchants were becoming richer. They sent their sons to schools to master mathematics for business careers and to learn about antiquity so that they could converse knowledgeably in social settings. (This was the mark of gentility.) They built huge city homes (palazzos) and country estates (villas) in the classical style, filling them with collections of ancient coins, vases, and statues. They competed among themselves to hire the best artists to beautify the churches, their private chapels, and their own imposing domiciles.

The ideals of the early humanists had grown into a whole new way of looking at life. What had begun as a scholarly interest in ancient literature had evolved into a cult of antiquity. Florence, proud of its independent spirit and its active community of artists and thinkers, hailed itself as the "new Athens." Academies, modeled on Cosimo's Platonic Academy, sprang up among elite communities throughout northern and central Italy. Pomponio Leto founded the Roman Academy, whose members met regularly for dinner to discuss classical topics. They addressed each other by Roman nicknames such as Marcus and Julius and they even wore togas!

Italian households did not dine on pizza and spaghetti with tomato sauce (tomatoes grew only in America until European explorers brought some back with them in the sixteenth century), but they enjoyed a number of dishes that are commonly served in today's Italian restaurants. Pasta was a basic part of most meals. Pasta noodles supposedly originated in the Tuscan city of Siena, green lasagna (pasta made with spinach juice) came from Bologna, and ravioli (filled pasta shells) was first served in Genoa. (Some historians believe that the concept of noodles was originally brought back from China by the Italian explorer Marco Polo.) Favorite sauces of the fourteenth century included pesto (ground pine nuts, basil, garlic and olive oil) and *panna* (which had a butter and cream base). Then as now, a popular soup was *minestrone*

(vegetables and pasta cooked in a chicken broth) And everyone, even children, drank the local wine. It was diluted with water.

Two meals a day were served: dinner at about 10 o'clock in the morning and supper (a lighter meal) at 5 PM. (Everyone had a very light breakfast when they first arose.) As you might expect, the

Pasta with pesto, still a favorite today

wealthy merchants enjoyed more exotic fare than the average family. They feasted upon such delicacies as guinea fowl, spiced veal, pork jelly, thrushes, pike, eel, trout, peacock, and turtle dove. Meat that was not fresh was strongly flavored with spices (pepper, cinnamon, cloves, nutmeg, saffron, which was extremely expensive, or ginger) imported from the East. The main purpose of the spices was to cover up the unpleasant taste of the rancid meat. There were no refrigerators in those days, so the meat was preserved with salt. After a while it had an awful taste, and this is when the spices came in handy! A favorite dessert of the wealthy was rice cooked in the milk of almonds served with sugar and honey. While the diners feasted on these delicacies, they were often entertained by a group of musicians.

Italians were eating with forks long before this useful utensil had been accepted in other parts of Europe. (The fork was a welcome improvement over eating with one's fingers.) When napkins were introduced in Florence in the fourteenth century, diners had to be advised not to spit into them or use them to blow their noses! Other dining etiquette of the time included rules against scratching oneself at the table (even the wealthy were afflicted with lice and fleas), cleaning the ears with one's fingers, or putting feet on the table. Imagine how terrible table manners must have been before these rules were made!

Wealthy merchants in the major cities often presided over festive Roman-inspired banquets. The entertainment was just as important as the food. Each new course was introduced by a fanfare of trumpets followed by music suggestive of the type of food about to be served. Platters of boar or venison were announced by the horns of hunters, fish dishes were introduced by songs about water, while wine called for lyrics about Bacchus (the Roman god of the vine). In between courses, the diners enjoyed classical poetry and dance. When it was time for desert, dwarfs, jugglers, or musicians were often carried into the hall in giant pastries, suddenly bursting out of them to the delight of all. As in ancient Rome, the banquets could go on for hours. The cook for the d'Este Court at Ferrara wrote that while the guests dipped their hands in perfumed water, singers and musicians provided background entertainment for the seventeenth course!

Of course, ordinary laborers ate more simply. The staple of their diet was bread (made from wheat, barley, or rye). This was often mixed with water and cabbage and cooked as a stew. Meat was very expensive and was only served on special occasions.

Lorenzo the Magnificent

Cosimo de Medidi was succeeded by his son, Piero "the Gouty," who was physically frail and soon died. Piero was succeeded by his son, Lorenzo (1449-1492). He was educated at the Platonic Academy and the recently established University of Florence. As a lad, Lorenzo had learned much about politics from his grandfather Cosimo, with whom he often played long games of chess. He later visited the ruins of ancient Rome with Alberti and marveled at the city's rich heritage. Lorenzo enjoyed talking with the artists who frequented the Medici palazzo and took an active interest in their theories. He learned to play several musical instruments (music was one of his passions) and composed poetry. In short, he was a gifted, well-educated young man, admirably equipped to follow in the footsteps of his legendary grandfather.

Later generations would know him as *Il Magnifico* ("The Magnificent"). Not that he looked the part. Lorenzo was rather unattractive, having a swarthy complexion, heavy features, a long, pointy noise, and a harsh, high-pitched voice. However, he was so charming that people soon forgot about his ungainly physical appearance.

Lorenzo was only twenty when he suddenly found himself the head of the Medici dynasty and in charge of the fate of Florence. Although the city was still technically a republic, Lorenzo would rule the government "from behind the scenes," just as Cosimo had once done. He was a skillful diplomat, and he made it a major goal to maintain peaceful relations with the other major city-states of Italy.

Peace didn't come right away, however. Not long after he took over the reins of power, Lorenzo's life was threatened by a conspiracy led by the powerful Pazzi family (banking rivals of the Medici) and supported by the wealthy Pitti

Statue of Lorenzo the Magnificent

who escaped were relentlessly hunted down. One was dragged home from Constantinople, and Lorenzo took personal satisfaction in sketching his execution. After the Pazzi Conspiracy, Lorenzo was always accompanied by ten armed bodyguards, one holding a drawn sword.

Jacopo de Pazzi, the patriarch of the Pazzi family, had opposed the conspiracy at first but was won over by the Pope. After Giuliano was murdered, Jacopo escaped to the village of Castagno, but the villagers recognized him and brought him back to Florence. There he was tortured, stripped naked, and hanged from the Palazzo della Signoria. He was later buried in Santa Croce, but he didn't rest in peace. A group of Florentines, blaming the recent heavy rains on his evil spirit, dug up the body and threw it into a ditch in an apple orchard. And this wasn't the end of it. The body was later removed and dragged through the streets of Florence by a mob shouting, "Make way for the great knight!" They propped up the rotting carcass against the Palazzo Pazzi, where the decomposing head was used as a door knocker! Eventually, the remains of poor Jacopo were thrown into the Arno River.

Among the first conspirators executed were an Archbishop and a young (teen-aged) cardinal. The cardinal's uncle was none other than the Pope. Now Sixtus really had something to be angry about. Seeking vengeance for his murdered nephew, he allied himself with King Ferdinand of Naples and began assembling an army of mercenaries to attack Florence. At this point Lorenzo set off, alone and unarmed, on a secret journey to Naples. He used his skills of diplomacy to charm Ferdinand, enticing him with a generous offer of gold florins if he (the King) would switch allegiances. This venture took great courage: Ferdinand had previously murdered more than one important guest! Fortunately, he accepted the

family and even by Pope Sixtus IV. (The Pope was angered by a clash between his business interests and the policies of the Medici bank.) Lorenzo and his brother, Giuliano, were attacked beneath Brunelleschi's dome as a priest was conducting Mass. Giuliano was stabbed to death, and Lorenzo narrowly escaped by hiding behind the famous bronze doors of the Sacristy.

As news of the attack spread throughout the city, the Florentines rallied in support of the Medici. Within hours most of the conspirators were hanging from the windows of the Palazzo della Signoria. A grateful Lorenzo commissioned the young artist Botticelli (more about him later) to depict their dangling bodies in a painting, and he had wax portraits of his dead brother placed at every street corner in Florence. Those conspirators

Medici Gardens

bribe and pulled out, forcing Sixtus to abandon his plans. A triumphant Lorenzo was toasted as a great hero by the greatly relieved citizens of Florence.

Like his grandfather, Lorenzo never held public office, but his advice and opinions were sought in every major government decision. Knowing that Florence could not compete with stronger powers on the battlefield, he maintained peace by forming alliances, lending money, and making gifts (actually, they were bribes). He masterminded extensive financial deals with many of the leaders of Europe. In medieval times monarchs had focused their energies on war; for them military victory meant glory and survival. But the men who ruled northern Italy in the fifteenth century knew that the key to success lay in skillful negotiation, and Lorenzo was a master at it.

Lorenzo did not share his grandfather's love of business, however, and because of his neglect the bank came close to collapsing on more than one occasion. (Lorenzo used public money to cover his losses.) He preferred the challenge of politics, and the profits he might have reinvested in the

family business were spent on his highly refined life style. Lorenzo loved to spend time at his several country estates. The extensive gardens of the villa at Careggi were laid out geometrically and planted with cypress and myrtle, the trees of antiquity. (The new theories of art even affected gardening!) Often he would stroll about the grounds, reading the descriptions by Roman poets Horace and Catallus of the Roman countryside. Every year on November 7 he held a banquet at the villa in honor of Plato's birth. Careggi became the gathering spot of a brilliant circle of poets, artists, and musicians.

Lorenzo started a school for sculptors in the garden of the Medici Palace in Florence. He employed a former pupil of Donatello to act as instructor and loaned him numerous paintings, antique busts and statues, which were set up in a studio and around the grounds. Like Cosimo, he continued to support the local churches and monasteries, but he concentrated his wealth on a private collection of ancient vases, cameos, bronze statuettes, jewels, and lavishly illustrated classical manuscripts. His vast collection of books became the first public library in Europe. (It was freely available to all.) But although he enjoyed learning about the ancient world, it was Dante and Boccaccio who inspired Lorenzo to compose lyrical verses about the countryside in the Tuscan vernacular.

Botticelli

Among the artists Lorenzo supported was Alessandro di Mariano dei Filipepi (1445-1510). He is known by his nickname, *Botticelli* (little barrels), a reference, perhaps, to his forebears who were coopers (barrel makers). Young Botticelli was apprenticed to a goldsmith, in whose workshop he developed a taste for the precise, incised line that would later characterize his art. In the 1460's he studied painting under the guidance of well-established artists Fra Filippo Lippi and Andrea del Verrocchio. These masters taught him how to paint solid looking figures and to contrast light and dark to create the illusion of roundness and depth. And yet, from the beginning Botticelli's figures were so much more graceful than those of his teachers. His emphasis upon line rather than physical substance endowed them with an ethereal, almost spiritual quality. Although he understood the importance of perspective, he never made it a crucial part of his works. As a result, the men and women in his paintings often seem to be drifting, in a most refined and elegant manner, through empty space. His unique style has been described as "pure visual poetry."

In the 1470's Botticelli was the darling of Lorenzo's brilliant circle. He painted *The Adoration of the Magi* as a sort of homage to the Medici family. It depicts Cosimo as a Wise Men kneeling before the infant Jesus. Lorenzo, with a haughty expression, stands to the left, looking on. They are dressed in the styles of their own age. This peculiar custom of placing wealthy patrons in contemporary attire among the traditional figures in biblical scenes became quite common during the Renaissance. The artist even included himself in the painting among the Magi. (You can see him in the right foreground, wearing a yellow robe and gazing right at you.) The Medici family had long promoted the family's connection with the Magi, whom they considered their patron saints. They sponsored a religious fraternity devoted to the Eastern sages, and on Epiphany family members processed through Florence in the role of the ancient kings. This probably inspired Botticelli's painting.

Adoration of the Magi

Primavera

The fascination with Greek deities among the people of Lorenzo's court is reflected in Botticelli's mythological paintings. The two most celebrated of these are *Primavera* (Spring) and *The Birth of Venus*. The first is an imaginative and dreamlike interpretation of the ancient legends associated with springtime. Nature is represented by the Roman goddess of spring (Flora), while the three graces (goddesses associated with poetry, music, and drama) symbolize the arts. This painting hung for years at the Medici villa at Castello. *The Birth of Venus* depicts the goddess of love and beauty arising from an enormous seashell. Like *Primavera*, it is filled with symbols designed to appeal to the sophisticated men of Lorenzo's court. For the

humanists, the birth of the goddess symbolized the rebirth of ancient forms of art.

Botticelli also painted a number of religious works, and in 1481 he created a series of drawings to illustrate an edition of Dante's *Divine Comedy*. Then, suddenly, he had nothing to do with the Medici. He painted no more blissful, elegant figures. Instead, his works took on a disturbing tone. The cause of this big change was a man named Savonarola.

Savonarola

Before we meet this infamous man, let's return to the story of Lorenzo de Medici. Since he was not inclined to devote too much time to the family business, the Medici bank began a long downward spiral. One by one, the branches in London, Bruges, and Milan had to be closed. In 1490 a number of factors (the most important one was an attack upon Italian traders by the Ottoman Turks) caused the Florentine economy to sag, and the local merchants unfairly blamed Lorenzo. They claimed that he spent too much time on his court and not enough on business. Suddenly, "Il Magnifico" was vulnerable.

This is when Girolamo Savonarola arrived on the scene. He was an Italian friar from the city-state of Ferrara, who became a fiery religious reformer. He had been invited in 1489 by a well-meaning Lorenzo to live at the recently rebuilt monastery of San Marco. Savonarola was so shocked by the opulence of Florence that he turned against the Medici family. A spell-binding preacher, Savonarola packed 10,000 people each Sunday into the Duomo to hear his tirades against the greed and materialism of the Florentines, and he demanded that Lorenzo account for his sinful ways. His sermons were so moving that his followers became known as the *Piagnoni* (the Weepers). Among them was Botticelli. No wonder his last paintings are so serious and religious in tone. The friar condemned parties, gambling, swearing, horse-racing, and anything else that he considered a corruption of Christian values. He urged the Florentine people to abandon all earthly pleasures, warning that if they did not heed his words a terrible crisis would befall the city.

Lorenzo died at Careggi in 1492 at the age of forty-three. That seems like a young age for a vigorous man to pass away, and it shouldn't have happened. All he had was an attack of gout, a slight fever, and a stomach infection - nothing life threatening. But his doctors "did him in" by forcing him to swallow a mixture of ground up pearls and precious stones that was supposed to cure his ills! As Lorenzo lay dying, Savonarola was summoned to issue the last rites, but the friar refused. When "Il Magnifico" died, Pope Innocent VIII remarked, "The peace of Italy is at an end."

The Pope certainly knew what he was talking about, because soon afterwards King Charles VIII of France attacked Florence, fulfilling Savonarola's awful prophecy of calamity. This did a lot to raise the Florentines' opinion of the frair. When Lorenzo's son, Piero, surrendered the city to him, the furious townspeople rebelled and ordered all the Medici out of town. Piero fled to Rome with his brothers, Giuliano and Giovanni (the future Pope Leo X, who was disguised as a friar). As Charles marched south from Florence to conquer other parts of Italy, Savonarola held the citizens in the palm of his hand, filling the vacuum of power by becoming the city's new ruler.

Statue of Savonarola

For four years the friar and his bands of armed disciples controlled Florence. He issued decrees calling for continual fasting and demanding the removal of all art treasures from the churches. He appointed squads ("Blessed Bands") of children, who spied on their parents and patrolled the streets, rebuking over-dressed women and denouncing gambling. In a huge "Bonfire of the Vanities" in the Piazza della Signoria, Savonarola's followers burned all the non-religious paintings they could find, as well as fancy clothing and ornaments, wigs and false beards, mirrors, pots of rouge, musical instruments, and classical books. Of course, there were some who opposed all this. Gangs of young dissenters, the *Arrabbiati* (the Angry) once snuck into the cathedral and filled the friar's pulpit with cow dung!

Savonarola believed that he could make Florence so holy that its example of piety would spread to the rest of Italy. Pope Alexander VI became alarmed by his excesses and excommunicated him for his fanatical behavior, but Savonarola ignored the papal bulls (written orders) and denounced the pontiff as an agent of Satan! He went on to criticize the immorality of the Pope (he had good reason to do so, as we will see), and predicted the ultimate punishment of the Catholic Church for the sinful acts of its leaders.

After four years, the Florentines grew weary of the friar's narrow-minded views and puritanical teachings. When the Pope placed the city under an interdict in an effort to shackle Savonarola (no church services could take place), a mob dragged the friar from his headquarters at San Marco. He was tried and condemned by a local court. On May 23, 1498 he was hanged for heresy in the Piazza della Signoria, near the site of his famous Bonfire of the Vanities. His body was then burned, and the ashes were thrown in the Arno.

Review Questions

1. Why were banks so important to the cloth merchants?

2. How did Cosimo differ from his father?

3. How is humanism reflected in the statues of Donatello?

4. What was the major technique that allowed Brunelleschi to construct the dome?

5. What is linear perspective?

6. How was Masaccio influenced by Donatello and Brunelleschi?

7. List three adjectives that describe the wealthy merchants of fifteenth century Florence.

8. How did Lorenzo deal with the men involved in the Pazzi conspiracy?

9. How did Botticelli's paintings differ from the other Renaissance works we have studied?

10. What was Savonarola's Bonfire of the Vanities?

Further Thoughts

1. The insignia of the Medici family was a cluster of red balls and one blue ball on a gold background. Its origins are a mystery. Some scholars believe that if the early Medici were

Medici coat of arms

pharmacists (as their name implies) the balls must represent pills. Others say that the circles are in fact benzants, coins from Byzantium (the same as appeared on the coat of arms of the Guild of Moneychangers to which the Medici belonged). But there is also the legend that the family was descended from Averardo, a brave knight who fought for Charlemagne. He had passed through Tuscany on his way to Rome and near Florence had come upon a savage giant, the terror of the poor peasants of the region. Averardo fought and killed the monster. During the fight his shield received several massive blows from the giant's mace. Charlemagne had rewarded Averardo's bravery by allowing him to commemorate his victory by representing the dents on his coat-of-arms by the six balls (*palle*) on a field of gold.

2. The frescoes of the Brancacci Chapel have narrowly escaped destruction. In 1680 the Marchese Francesco Ferroni tried to take over the patronage of the chapel and ordered his men to "get rid of these ridiculous men in their cassocks and old-fashioned outfits." Grand Duchess Vittoria della Rovera prevented their removal. Then in 1771 a fire burned down most of the church, but fortunately the chapel survived.

3. Carnival was a festival celebrated by all classes of society in the towns and cities of Italy. Everyone put on masks and pretended to be someone else, and the crowds filled the streets to dance, drink, sing, and eat "carnivorously" (hence the term "carnival"). In the time of Lorenzo the Magnificent the Florentine Carnival was noted for its extravagant spectacles, parades, and processions. Lorenzo even wrote music for some of the events.

Projects

1. Write an essay comparing Cosimo de Medici to Augustus of ancient Rome.

2. Two Medici women became queens of France. Catherine married Henry II, and was mother of three French kings. Marie married Henry IV, and was mother of Louis XIII. Two Medici men became popes: Leo X and Clement VII. Choose one of these famous family members and write a report.

3. The Platonic Academy was inspired by Plato's Academy, which was established in Athens in the fourth century BC. Find out more about this early gathering spot for scholars. Then do some research on the Platonic Academy. Think about what you've learned. Now write a short report, comparing the two academies.

4. Donatello perfected the bronze casting technique. Find out the various steps involved in casting a statue in bronze. Then make a poster or graphic design to illustrate them.

5. Verrochio was a master sculptor in his own right. One of his greatest works was his bronze statue of David. Consult an art book and find an illustration of the statue. Then write a paragraph or two comparing it to Donatello's DAVID.

6. The next time you go to an Italian restaurant closely study the menu. Which dishes might have been served during the early Renaissance (fourteenth and fifteenth centuries). Which ones couldn't possibly have been? Write a short summary of your findings.

7. Search the Internet to find a description of Botticelli's *Primavera*. Read the commentary. Then turn to the illustration of the painting on page 80 and identify the various figures. Explain what each figure symbolizes.

8. Paolo Ucello loved perspective. Find out more about this Italian painter and write a short report.

Botticelli's Portrait of a Lady

CHAPTER 5

THE HIGH RENAISSANCE

In the mid-sixteenth century, Italian painter and architect Giorgio Vasari wrote a monumental book, entitled *The Lives Of The Most Imminent Italian Architects, Painters And Sculptors*. Modeled upon ancient Greek and Roman biographies of famous men, Vasari's *Lives* was carefully researched and included his own critical judgments. This was the first major work to concentrate exclusively on the history of art, and, despite a number of inaccuracies, it became the standard reference on the Italian Renaissance for the next two centuries.

Vasari's Ideas

The whole concept of the *renaissance* (French for "rebirth") of art was invented by Vasari. He divided the evolution of this rebirth into three stages corresponding to the childhood, youth, and maturity of a human being. Vasari believed that art was reborn in Italy in the late thirteenth century, when Cimabue, Giotto and the Pisani broke away from the Middle Ages and ushered in the "good modern manner." He wrote, "...painters owe a debt to Giotto...the same debt they owe to nature."

The works of Donatello, Brunelleschi, and Masaccio represented the youth of the revival of western art, and the great artists of the sixteenth century brought it to its maturity, its "Golden Age." At last, Vasari marveled, the works of Leonardo da Vinci, Michelangelo, Raphael, and Titian reached a state of perfection that exceeded the models of classical antiquity.

Vasari's Golden Age of Italian art is known to modern scholars as the High Renaissance. It was during this exciting period that the innovations of the earlier masters we have been studying found their fullest expression. While admiring the harmony, grace, and balance of ancient art, the artists of the High Renaissance went far beyond copying the works of the past. What began as an attempt to represent the physical world as realistically as possible evolved into a belief that nature could, and even should, be improved upon by the imagination and talents of the artist. The paintings and statues of the High Renaissance depict handsome, idealized men and women who embody the elegance and refinement of the age. While the figures of Masaccio are standing or sitting quietly, those of the new generation of artists move freely, often straining every muscle. By this time, competence in such techniques as linear perspective and chiaroscuro was taken for granted. Art had certainly come a long way since the Middle Ages, when its main function was to tell a biblical story. Now it was not the end (purpose) but the means (method) that counted, and a fine painting was valued simply for what it was, not what it meant.

Leonardo da Vinci

Vasari began his section on the Golden Age in his book with Leonardo da Vinci (1452-1519), describing him as a divinely endowed genius who ranks among the angels. Leonardo was born near the small hamlet of Vinci, east of Florence. He had little formal education and spent much of his childhood frolicking in the wooded hillsides of Tuscany. At the age of seventeen he began an apprenticeship in the workshop of painter Andrea del Verrocchio, one of the bright stars of Lorenzo's court.

Verrocchio was a goldsmith, engineer, and sculptor as well as a painter. He instructed Leonardo to carefully observe the tiniest details of nature and to include them in his paintings. However, it was Giotto and Masaccio who inspired the young apprentice to paint lifelike figures. According to legend, Verrocchio once asked Leonardo to add an angel to a painting he was working on (*The Baptism Of Christ*). Leonardo obliged and created a figure that was so realistic and emotionally appealing that Verrocchio decided to give up painting and concentrate on sculpture for the rest of his career!

In 1472 Leonardo became a master painter in the Guild of Saint Luke. (Saint Luke was the patron saint of painters.) He experimented with new techniques to create the illusion of the third dimension (depth or perspective) and discovered that he could make objects appear to recede into the distance simply by diminishing the degree of detail and the intensity of color - objects in the distance appear in shades of blue. He dabbled with chiaroscuro and tried softening the edges of the images in a painting so that the colors and tones gradually shifted from light to dark without clear cut lines or demarcations. This technique, known as *sfumato*, made the figures seem to emerge from the background. (*Sfumato* means smoke in Italian, and it refers to the hazy area between object and background.) He also observed that shadows come in colors; artists traditionally painted all shadows grey, but Leonardo painted a shadow on snow blue, one in the grass dark green, and generally painted the shadow a darker shade than the setting itself. These various techniques helped Leonardo to create scenes that were so believable that Vasari claimed he had "endowed his figures with motion and breath."

Unlike the earlier artists we have studied, Leonardo usually used oil paints. The idea of mixing powdered pigments with oil to make paint was not new: artists in ancient Greece, Rome and Byzantium mixed vegetable oils with their paint pigments, but the concept had been forgotten until Flemish artists began mixing the powders with linseed oil. The old tempera pigments were gradually abandoned by most Italian artists after 1470, when Antonello da Messina brought the new medium of oils to Venice.

A major advantage of oil paint is that it dries more slowly than tempera, giving the artist more time to work on small details. (Remember how quickly the egg yolk in tempera dried?) Colors could be blended right on the panel, and this produced a continuous scale of hues that included rich, velvety dark shades never seen in a fresco.

LEONARDO DA VINCI

Statue of Leonardo

Oils enabled the artist to create a wide range of visual sensations - the glitter of gold, the sheen of silk or satin, the deep pile of fur, the sparkle of jewels, the softness of velvet, the delicacy of lace, and even the wrinkles and blemishes of the human face. Different thicknesses, varying from a thin, translucent film (known as a glaze) to the thickest material (called impasto) could be applied to make objects appear to stand out or recede into the background.

The Adoration Of The Magi (this was certainly a popular theme) was Leonardo's first large group painting. Although this unfinished panel contains only the under drawing (like a cartoon), it shows us that, from the beginning, Leonardo applied principles of mathematics and geometry to the planning of his works. The figures in this painting are arranged among deep shadows in a pyramid shape so that our eyes are drawn to the principal subject, the Holy Child. The figures in this scene were traditionally painted in profile, with Mary and the Child on one side of the picture and the kings on the other. Leonardo's subjects look directly at you, making them more interesting and the drama of the moment more compelling. Leonardo frequently left his paintings unfinished, as he did with this one. He had an extremely curious mind, as we will soon see, and he often dropped one project when a new challenge appeared. Of those paintings he completed only twelve have survived.

At the age of thirty, Leonardo went to Milan to work for Ludovico Sforza. Ludovico was descended from Francesco Sforza, the condottiere who had seized power from the Visconti. Because Ludovico's authority depended upon his army, Leonardo recommended himself for a position in his court by drawing plans for collapsible bridges, machines for draining trenches, siege equipment, armored cars, and multi-barreled guns (ancestors of the modern machine gun). As an afterthought, he briefly described his peacetime activities - architecture, sculpting, and painting! He got the job and spent seventeen years in Milan. Much of his time was devoted to designing costumes, scenery, and revolving stages for court plays. However, he did paint a portrait of Ludovico's young mistress (*Lady With An Ermine*) and a uniquely staged *Madonna Of The Rocks*.

In 1495 he began his masterpiece, *The Last Supper* - a fresco decorating the wall of the refectory (dining hall) of the monastery of Santa Maria delle Grazie. With a masterful blending of light and shadow, he dramatized the twelve disciples' reaction to Christ's startling announcement, at a Passover feast, that one of them would betray him. Each man responds in a different way Judas, the culprit, guiltily leans away into the shadows. Leonardo often used gesture to reflect inner feelings, having noted that "painted figures ought to be done in such a way that those who see them will be able to easily recognize from their attitudes the thoughts of their minds." His mathematical approach to design is reflected in the way the disciples are arranged in neat divisions of two groups of six, each group subdivided in half. In earlier paintings of this subject, the disciples simply sat in a long line behind the table, looking forward, with Christ in the center. Leonardo's groupings are much more natural. (Think about it. At a large family dinner, do we all sit in a row behind the table and stare straight ahead? Of course not! Each person interacts with the relatives seated nearby.)

Leonardo worked long hours on *The Last Supper*, often forgetting to eat. He frequently walked the streets of Milan, looking for faces upon which to model the disciples. Some days he did no painting at all. The prior of the monastery complained that he would come in, stare at the fresco for two hours, make six brush strokes and leave. Reacting to this criticism, Leonardo remarked that he was having difficulty visualizing the face of Judas, but if the prior was in a great hurry, his own (the prior's) face would do very well!

He was always experimenting with materials. Wishing to work more slowly on the fresco than wet plaster and tempera would allow, he applied a solution of tempera mixed with oil to dry plaster. The results were disastrous. Almost immediately the paint started to peel. Today, after repeated attempts at restoration, *The Last Supper* survives only as a magnificent ruin.

While in Milan Leonardo designed a bronze equestrian statue of Ludovico's father, Francesco. (Do you remember who made the first Renaissance equestrian statue?) This was to be the largest bronze statue ever made, but after six years he had produced only a huge clay model of the horse. When the French invaded Milan (more about this in a later chapter), the many tons of bronze that had been put aside for the statue were snatched away by the government and used to make guns. Adding insult to injury, French archers used the clay model for target practice and totally destroyed it!

Returning to Florence after the French invasion, Leonardo began work on his portrait of *Mona Lisa* (*My Lady Lisa*). This is probably the most famous painting in the world today. According to Vasari, Lisa was the wife of a Florentine nobleman. Leonardo wanted to avoid the melancholic look so often seen in the portraits of his day, so he hired musicians and buffoons to entertain Lisa and make her smile. (Actually, perhaps from shyness, she only offered the mysterious half smile that has made her so famous.) He painted more of her torso than was customary in portraits (a painting usually included only the face and upper chest), and he arranged her folded hands in such a way that, once again, he had formed a pyramid drawing our attention to the focal point, her face. Leonardo's

Mona Lisa

mastery of sfumato and chiaroscuro make Lisa appear to be moving out of the darkness. This painting was a personal favorite of the artist. He kept it with him wherever he lived, and it was at his bedside when he died. Today it is displayed in the Louvre Museum in Paris. As you enter the room, the lady seems to follow you with her eyes, quietly laughing to herself.

Leonardo wanted to understand everything he could about the natural world so that his art would be as realistic as possible. He was constantly asking himself questions. Why were sea shells found in the mountains? How were the locks in Flanders designed? What causes cracks in walls? What is the origin of clouds and wind? How does a body function? By studying the smallest structural details of an object, he believed that he could learn how it functioned. He was fascinated by the flight of birds. Although he was a vegetarian, he often went to the town market to buy live birds. He set them loose in a closed room and studied their movements. When he was done, he set them free.

He dissected over thirty corpses to better understand human anatomy (until Pope Leo X barred him from the mortuary in Rome). Once, having discovered a centenarian (a hundred-year-old man) in a hospital in Florence, he patiently awaited the old man's demise so that he could examine his ancient veins. Leonardo made detailed drawings showing the make-up of bones, tendons, and muscles, and he accurately explained their functions. He considered the human body to be the ultimate machine, and he used it as a model for many mechanical devices. For example, he analyzed the tendons of the hand to design a keyboard and the upper larynx to make a musical recorder. He was fascinated by deformities as much as by beauty. He once got a band of peasants drunk so he could sketch their glassy-eyed facial expressions!

Leonardo recorded most of his observations in a series of 116 notebooks, which he planned to be the basis of an encyclopedic work about nature. Over 7,000 pages of the voluminous books still exist. (Two notebooks were discovered as recently as 1965.) They are written in a peculiar right-to-left script, which must be read using a mirror. Scattered among the descriptions are sketches and preliminary drawings of many of his paintings as well as mathematical puzzles, the detailed studies of bones, muscles, and wings we have just learned about, and drawings of such inventions as diving helmets, musical instruments, a life jacket, a parachute, and the lock gates for a canal. There are also designs of all sorts of machines: a military tank, a human powered flying machine, ball-bearing mechanisms, steam cannons, machine guns, a mechanical digger, steam engines, a car powered by springs, and cranes.

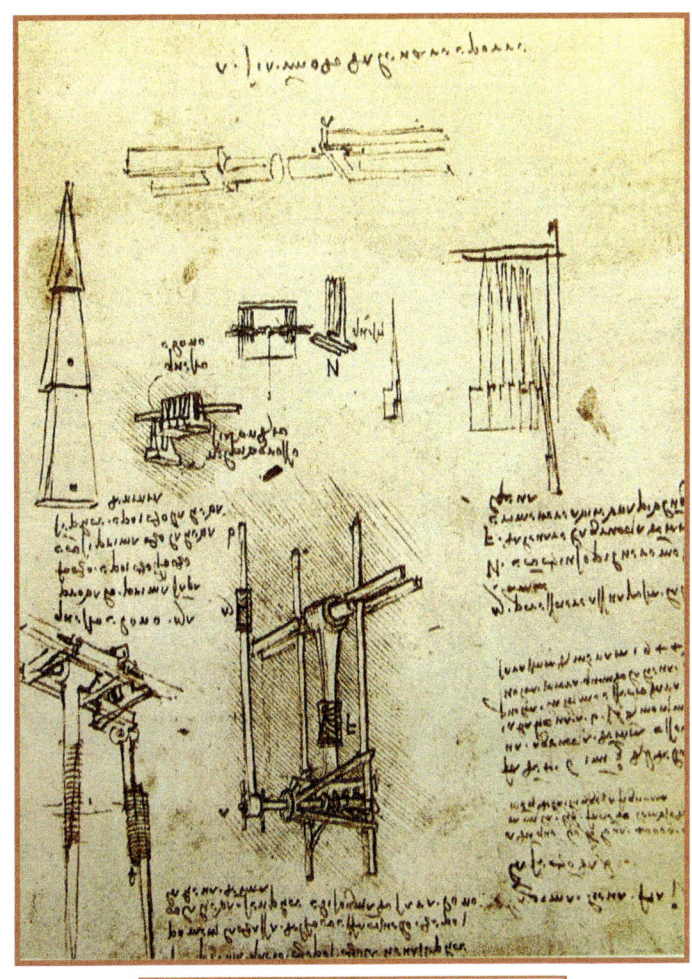

A page from Leonardo's notebooks

Many of Leonardo's machines would never have worked in practice, but his ideas were far more advanced and imaginative than those of his contemporaries. Some of his projects had great potential: his flying machine was a prototype for our modern hang glider. He also proposed that the sun does not move, a radical view in those days when leading scientists (and the Church) insisted that the sun revolves around the earth. Few people took this idea seriously. Later in the century, Copernicus would come to the same conclusion and stir up a great deal of controversy. But that time had not yet come. Because Leonardo routinely performed experiments to find out why things happened, he is regarded by many as the founder of modern science. He proudly signed one collection of his writings, "Leonardo, disciple of experiment."

This artistic and scientific genius spent his last years working at the French court of Francis I, arranging fireworks displays and designing clever devices for pageants and parades. He made a mechanical lion for the king that took a few steps forward and then opened its breast to reveal a mass of white lilies, the symbol of France. It is a sad commentary that the finest mind of his age was reduced to making gadgets for bored courtiers. Leonardo's talents were appreciated by only a handful of his contemporaries, and when he died, his notebooks lay forgotten in an attic. It was not until Vasari's book appeared fifty years later that he was acknowledged as one of the greatest men who ever lived.

The Restoration of Papal Authority

Let's take a step or two back in time. Do you remember the Great Schism of the Church when there were two popes -one in Rome and one in Avignon, France? After the Papacy was restored in Rome in 1417, Pope Martin V took the first steps toward strengthening the authority and dignity of the Catholic Church. By the end of his term he had wrestled control of the Papal States from the local nobility and begun the clean-up of the city of Rome. Two decades later, a group of rebellious barons drove Martin's successor, Pope Eugene IV, from Rome. (He fled down the Tiber River in a rowboat, disguised as a monk.) The Pope found refuge in the Florence of Cosimo de Medici, and that city became his headquarters for nine years.

Eugene was mightily impressed by the ideas and accomplishments of the humanists he encountered in Florence, and when he finally returned to Rome, he invited Donatello and several others to accompany him. He also employed Flavio Biondo, a historian and archaeologist, as papal secretary. Biondi catalogued the surviving monuments of ancient Rome in three encyclopedic volumes, and, using relics, inscriptions, and early chronicles, he wrote lively descriptions of the manners and customs of Imperial Rome. His works encouraged the development of chorography (the study of local history from surviving remains). After Biondo's efforts, generations of excavators engaged by succeeding popes would unearth all sorts of fascinating ancient ruins and artifacts.

In 1447 a humanist scholar named Tommaso Parentucelli was elected Pope Nicholas V. He was a highly motivated and energetic little man who loved books. As an impoverished monk he had gone into debt collecting the works of classical writers. He once advised Cosimo de Medici on texts to obtain for his expanding library. Nicholas was convinced that the values and ideals of the ancients could pump fresh life into Christianity, so he hired dozens of scholars to copy classical texts, while his agents scoured Europe in pursuit of rare volumes. His collection of 9,000 books and manuscripts (all bound in red velvet with silver clasps) formed the nucleus of the Vatican Library. It would become the greatest library in the western world.

Nicholas was the first pope to envision a revival of the grandeur of ancient Rome. He set in motion a major restoration of the decaying city, ordering the streets to be repaired and the worst slums to be demolished. He consulted Alberti for the reconstruction of the city's crumbling bridges and aqueducts, and he had the foundations laid for a new papal palace on Vatican Hill. Nicholas held a jubilee in Rome in 1450 to attract pilgrims to visit the city. (Their offerings would enrich his building fund.) Over 100,000 people came, and so many crowded on to the main bridge across the Tiber River that it collapsed! Unfortunately, much of the revival of Rome led to the progressive destruction of the ancient ruins, as temples and other structures were looted for their stone. Workmen removed over 2,000 wagon loads of marble from the famous Colosseum in a single year. They also quarried the fine stone from the Circus Maxiums, the Forum, the Arch of Titus, and the Temple of Venus.

During the rule of Nicholas, the Ottoman Turks overthrew Constantinople (in 1453), an act the Pope considered to be as much a blow to scholarship as to religion. As it turned out he was wrong, since scholars fleeing from the Byzantine capital would dramatically enrich the humanist movement in the West.

Sixtus IV came to power in 1471. Another scholarly theologian, he donated over 1,000 Greek and Latin manuscripts to the Vatican Library (which he opened to all interested scholars). He improved everyday life in Rome by constructing many more new roads and bridges, and by having the ancient pipes and aqueducts cleaned and restored to a functioning state, thus providing an abundant supply of cold, clear water. He built the Sistine Chapel, which he named after himself. Its proportions are the same as those of Solomon's Temple described in the Book of Kings in the Bible. Sixtus also established the Sistine choir, which would help to make Rome a center of sacred music.

Not all of the Pope's activities were admirable, however. He placed many of his relatives in high positions of the Church. (He made five nephews and one grand-nephew cardinals.) The practice of basing appointments upon family connections is known as nepotism. It is never a popular practice, since the appointees are not necessarily qualified for the position. This was certainly true with the Pope's nephews, and his appointments led to a great deal of opposition among the other clergy, as well as among the ordinary parishioners. Sixtus even made his uneducated twenty-year-old servant the Bishop of Parma. He was the Pope who supported the Pazzi Conspiracy against Lorenzo the Magnificent, basically because it was in the best business interest of his family.

In 1492 Pope Calixtus followed Sixtus' example and promoted his ambitious and self-serving nephew, Rodrigo Borgia (a Spaniard), to a high position in the Church. Borgia later became Pope Alexander VI by bribing the cardinals to vote for him. He then spent much of his time promoting the interests of his family (he had several illegitimate children). He married his daughter, Lucrezia, to three of Italy's rulers, (one at a time!), and supported the efforts of his son, Cesare, to carve out a kingdom of his own among the Papal States. We'll learn more about Alexander's famous offspring later in our story.

Julius II and Leo X Glorify Rome

By the dawn of the sixteenth century, the population of Rome had expanded to 100,000. Julius II, a nephew of Sixtus IV, became Pope in 1503. He was a clever politician and a fine soldier, who personally led his armies into battle to protect the Papal States from invaders and to restore the Papacy's temporal (political) power. (His military campaigns earned him the nickname, "the warrior pope.") Believe it or not, he was sixty when he first wore the papal mantle. Julius allegedly vowed not to shave until he managed to rid Italy of all usurpers. His portraits reveal that he always had a long beard.

In 1508 Julius began an ambitious plan to beautify Rome as a means of glorifying his own image. He convinced wealthy citizens to build impressive palaces, churches, and public buildings by promising them tremendous tax concessions. When portions of the city were excavated to make room for new structures, a large number of ancient Roman artifacts were unearthed. These were gathered to form the papal collection of antique sculpture, to which Julius added the now famous *Apollo Belvedere* and *Laocoon* statues. The *Apollo*, a Roman copy of a Greek statue of the Olympian god, was made in the fourth century and discovered in his family vineyard when Julius was still a cardinal. *The Laocoon*, a Greek statue of a Trojan priest and his sons struggling with two snakes, was made in the first century BC. It was discovered in 1506 in another vineyard near the ancient Baths of Trajan in Rome. These two highly realistic ancient statues strongly influenced the artists who came to Rome to view them.

Julius chose architect Donato Bramante to direct his vast building program. Trained as a painter, Bramante had turned to architecture at

Laocoon

Apollo Belvedere

the Milanese court of Ludovico Sforza. He was there at the same time as Leonardo and shared his interest in geometric patterns. From the beginning, Bramante's buildings reflect his enchantment with the harmonious proportions of classical design. His first major work in Rome was the *Tempietto* (little temple), a small domed structure built on the spot where Saint Peter was crucified. It was the first Renaissance building to imitate the form of a circular ancient temple, and it became a prototype for sixteenth century church design.

Bramante's first commission for Julius was a series of classically inspired courtyards and galleries connecting the old Belvedere Palace of Pope Innocent VIII with the buildings of the Vatican Palace. He designed a wide spiral staircase within the tower that serves as an entrance to the papal palace. It could be ridden up on horseback in case of emergency. Because Bramante used marble from

The Tempietto

the local ancient ruins, he came to be known by many as "Ruinante!"

All this building activity inspired Julius to replace the old church of Saint Peter, which now seemed too dilapidated and old-fashioned for the times. The church had originally been constructed in 325 by Roman Emperor Constantine on the site of the alleged grave of Saint Peter. Bramante was commissioned to design the new church. The foundation stone was laid in 1506.

Bramante's design was based upon a Greek cross. (Because the four arms of the Greek cross were of equal length, architects considered it an ideal form.) A major dome was to be built over the center, with minor domes and bell towers at the ends of the four arms. (If this reminds you of the Byzantine churches, you have an excellent memory!) Unfortunately, the death of Julius in 1513 and that of Bramante the following year prevented the work from progressing much beyond the planning stage. But it was a start.

The rebuilding of Saint Peter's would occupy ten architects for a period of 120 years. When completed, it would be the largest church in the Christian world.

Pope Leo X was the second son of Lorenzo the Magnificent. He was educated by humanist scholars and made a cardinal when he was eighteen. (It was Leo who escaped from Florence with his brothers, when the city was attacked by the French.) He was a bull-necked, pop-eyed, red-faced, fat man. But although he lacked the charm of Julius and Alexander, he was quite sophisticated in his tastes, as you might expect from Lorenzo's offspring. When he became Pope at the age of thirty-seven, Leo allegedly told a friend, "Let us enjoy the Papacy/" His goal was to duplicate the glittering court of his father in the Vatican Palace, but on a far grander scale.

Leo patronized a wide circle of artists, scholars, and musicians, and he continued Julius' pet project - the construction of Saint Peter's. He spent so much on building new structures and tearing down old medieval ones in Rome that he nearly emptied the papal treasury. Fortunately, unlike his predecessors, he tried to preserve the ancient ruins. Leo loved to read, and he accumulated great numbers of books and manuscripts, which he added to the Vatican Library. He also set up a Greek school and expanded the university in Rome until it had more than 100 teachers.

Michelangelo

Let's return to Julius II. Some people remember him only as the patron of Michelangelo Buonarroti (1475-1564), a Florentine sculptor, painter, poet, and architect. Vasari described Michelangelo as the genius "who surpasses them all" (even Leonardo). Many modern art critics also view him as the supreme Renaissance artist. He was fascinated by the beauty and strength of the human body, which he believed to reflect the nobility of the human spirit. His art is not just an imitation of nature but an idealized, deeply personal vision of mankind.

Engraving of Michelangelo

Michelangelo was apprenticed to the highly respected painter, Domenico Ghirlandaio, and he later attended the art school established by Lorenzo de Medici. There he studied ancient sculptures under the guidance of the aged Bertaldo di Giovanni (Donatello's former pupil). The young artist was a perfectionist, and he often denigrated the work of Pietro Torrigiano, a fellow student in Lorenzo's school. On one occasion, Pietro become so enraged by the constant criticism that he broke his tormentor's nose!

Michelangelo's father, a wealthy man, had at first opposed his becoming an artist. Although the works of painters and sculptors were greatly admired in the fifteenth century, no member of the upper classes wanted his son to enter the trade. Fortunately, Lorenzo stepped in and convinced the elder Buonarroti to give his son a chance. In the years that followed, the status of the artist in society would dramatically improve.

There is a legend about Lorenzo coming upon Michelangelo in the villa garden as he was carving a statue. He asked what it was and was told it was "an old faun." (A faun is a Roman mythological figure that is half man and half goat.) Lorenzo then remarked that it didn't look old because its teeth were too good. Without thinking twice, the young sculptor knocked out one of the faun's front teeth with his chisel! Lorenzo was as amused by this irreverent act as he was impressed by the quality of the statue, so he invited the lad to move into his villa as a member of his household. Thus, at the age of only fourteen, Michelangelo found himself at the center of the Italian art world. He remained there for four years, polishing his artistic skills while mingling with some of the leading poets, artists, and philosophers of the day.

When Lorenzo died Michelangelo returned home, only to be unsettled by the teachings of Savonarola and worried about the friar's prophecy of impending doom. Unlike the humanists, who celebrated the power and potential of mankind, Michelangelo viewed man as a lonely and unhappy creature, the victim of circumstances beyond his control. This pessimistic attitude was a product of the artist's introspective temperament. Unlike the sociable and outgoing Leonardo da Vinci, Michelangelo was a brooding fellow, never content to rely upon others because he believed that he could do everything better himself. Often he did not complete a project because it was too ambitious and he was unwilling to ask for help.

While living in Florence, he found a way to study human anatomy. He made a deal with the prior of the local monastery of Santo Spirito, agreeing to carve a wooden crucifix for the church if he could dissect corpses in the abbey's cloisters. The knowledge of the muscles, bones, and organs of the body he obtained from these dissections would help him to create extremely realistic figures. He later traveled to Venice and then to Bologna, where he spent a year as the guest of a nobleman. His host introduced him to the works of Dante, Petrarch, and Boccaccio, and even encouraged him to write poetry.

The Pieta

In 1498 Michelangelo was commissioned by a cardinal in Rome to carve *The Pieta*, a sculpture of the Virgin Mary cradling the dead body of her son, Christ, after it was taken down from the cross. Look at an illustration of this statue. The life-like figures show how much the sculptor had learned about human anatomy. The limpness of Christ's

body is emphasized by the gentle folds of his mother's drapery. The pyramid shape of the two figures draws our attention to the apex - the face of Mary. (Leonardo, of course, had accomplished the same thing with a paintbrush.) Can you sense the tenderness and sadness in her youthful face? Unlike other artists, Michelangelo believed that the Virgin should appear as a young mother. When criticized about this, he replied that Mary's purity had protected her from the effects of aging. Besides, he remembered his own mother, who had died young. Mary raises her left hand. Does this express her resignation or her questioning of her son's terrible fate?

The Pieta is the only work Michelangelo ever signed. According to legend, he once overheard a nobleman remark that such a young sculptor could never have created such a marvelous piece of art. That night he carved his name on the stone to prove that he had! During this early period Michelangelo also carved a larger-than-life statue of Bacchus, the Roman god of wine. The drunken face and swaying pose of the young god create a sensation worlds apart from the grief expressed in *The Pieta*.

One of Michelangelo's major challenges came from the directors of the Duomo in Florence. In 1501 they commissioned him to carve a monumental statue of the biblical hero, David. The dimensions of the statue were dictated by a massive, but shallow, block of pure white marble quarried in 1466. A figure of a giant had been chiseled out of the block by a second-rate sculptor, botched, and then abandoned. Imagine how difficult it must have been to carve something original out of someone else's figure. If he succeeded, Michelangelo's statue would be fourteen feet high, the largest free-standing marble statue since classical times.

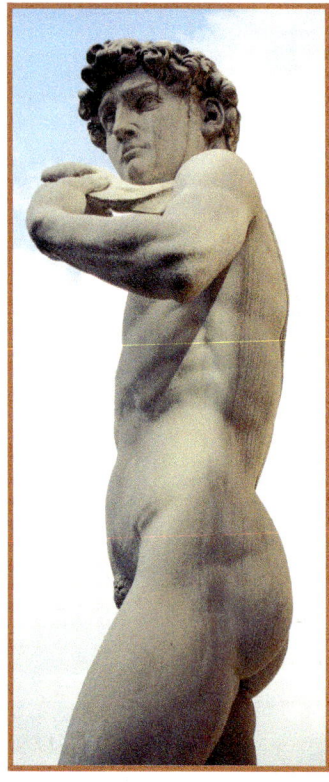

David

He took on the project enthusiastically, and when he finished, Vasari proclaimed that he had "worked a miracle in restoring to life something that had been left for dead." David stands defiantly with his sling over his shoulder, determined to defeat the formidable giant, Goliath. He appears calm (standing in contrapposto position), yet his muscles ripple and his veins pulse with tension. The statue is a hymn to Michelangelo's vision of the beauty, grace, and controlled strength of a great hero. It was such a hit in Florence that it was installed in front of the Palazzo della Signoria, where it represented the fiercely independent spirit of Florence. Vasari's final comment on the statue was succinct: "Anyone who has seen Michelangelo's *David* has no need to see anything else by any other sculptor, living or dead."

In 1505 Julius II asked Michelangelo

to paint the ceiling of the Sistine Chapel with a pictorial cycle of biblical history, from the creation of Adam to the coming of Moses. It would be the artist's greatest achievement. Working alone, he spent four and a half years painting a huge tableau of his own design. Vasari wrote that he labored in great discomfort, "having to work with his face looking upwards, which impaired his sight so

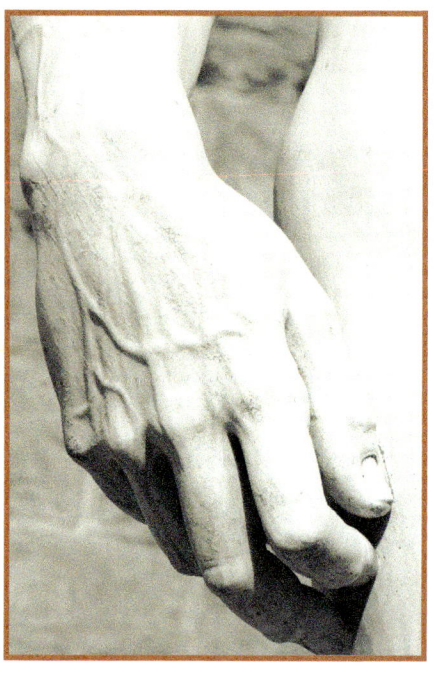

badly that he could not read or look at drawings save with his head turned backwards."

The ceiling posed an enormous challenge. To cover its vast expanse, he laid out an imposing, powerful structure of imaginary architecture and then filled its sections with 340 figures in nine scenes from Genesis and twelve from the New Testament. Gigantic likenesses of Old Testament prophets and ancient sibyls (female seers) sit upon thrones around the edges and between the scenes. They are included because they had prophesied the birth of Christ. Scholars believe that the prophet Moses is a portrait of Julius. The focal point of the tableau is the *Creation Of Adam*, in which the contact of fingers symbolizes God's gift of life to the reclining figure of the first man. Michelangelo

Michelangelo had created a swirling motion of activity around the central figure of Christ. In the lower left the dead are torn from their graves and carried by wingless angels toward the center to be judged by Christ. The righteous continue upward to join the ranks of the blessed in heaven, while the contorted bodies of the damned are hurled below, their faces filled with anguish and despair as they contemplate the horrible fate that awaits them in hell. Several pathetic sinners are knocked out of Charon's boat with the angry blow of an oar. (In Greek mythology Charon was the ferryman who transported the spirits of the dead across the River Styx.) Once again we have an interesting mingling of pagan and Christian traditions. Christ himself is depicted as young and vigorous, resembling the classical god Apollo, half rising from his seat to separate the just from the fallen. He is flanked by the Virgin Mary and the martyred saints.

constantly complained as he worked on the ceiling that he was a sculptor, not a painter. So be it. The figures of the vast fresco are so solid-looking and realistic that they seem to have been carved out of paint.

The major work of his later years was *The Last Judgment* on the altar wall of the Sistine Chapel. Julius had suggested that Michelangelo decorate the wall after completing the ceiling, but nothing more came of it. One of his successors, Paul III, commissioned the artist to take on the task. It was another huge area (covering 1,800 square feet), the largest ever tackled for a single work without any kind of subdividing framework (as was the case on the ceiling). Once again, Michelangelo took on the challenge, and when the fresco was unveiled in 1541 the Pope fell to his knees in awe.

Michelangelo's self-portrait can be seen in the skin held by Saint Bartholomew (who was flayed alive).

This fearsome vision of the Final Judgment provoked instant controversy. Much of the criticism was focused upon the nudity of the vast majority of the figures. (This was considered unsuitable for a religious subject.) While the work

Central figures of the Last Judgment

was still in progress one critic had complained that the figures were "better suited to the baths and taverns than among the heavenly chorus." Michelangelo responded by painting the face of the critic on his figure of the donkey-eared Midas, the mythical Greek king who appears as the judge in hell! Others objected that Christ was beardless and seemed too young.

The next Pope, Paul IV, urged Michelangelo to "tidy up" the fresco, to which the artist replied that the Pope should first tidy up the world and the painting would follow suit! Shortly before Michelangelo's death, a second-rate painter named Daniele da Volterra would be commissioned to provide draperies for the principal nudes. (This

earned him the nickname *Braghettone* - "breeches maker"). Even more clothing was painted on in later centuries. These attempts to add respectability harmed much of Michelangelo's painting and made recent attempts to restore it difficult.

While working on *The Last Judgment*, Michelangelo had time to sculpt a bust of Brutus, the leader of a conspiracy that killed Julius Caesar. (Brutus, you may recall, was one of the three villains of history whom Dante assigned to the jaws of Satan.) Michelangelo's portrait of the perfidious traitor (Caesar had treated him like a son) was inspired by the imperial busts of ancient Rome. Many consider *Brutus* to be an idealized portrait of Lorenzino de Medici, who killed his cousin, the Duke Alessandro, in 1537, attracting all the anti-Medici sympathizers of Florence to his side. Like many of Michelangelo's other statues, this one was left unfinished. (Another sculptor, Tiberio Calcagni, later carved the drapery and finished the neck and chin.)

In 1535 Michelangelo was appointed chief painter, sculptor, and architect of the Vatican Palace. He devoted his final years to the construction of Saint Peter's Cathedral. Bramante had designed a dome that was considered too massive and heavy. Michelangelo studied Brunelleschi's dome in Florence and then designed a taller, more pointed version. Like Brunelleschi's dome, his would have a double shell. The ribbed inner shell would be made of wood and the outer shell would consist of wood and lead. The structure would rise 435 feet.

The dome of Saint Peter's Cathedral

Raphael

Raffaello Sanzio (1483-1520) was perhaps the best loved artist of the High Renaissance. Raphael (he is known by the Anglicized version of his name) was a native of Urbino. He was apprenticed in the workshop of the well-respected painter Perugino and was later invited to the court of the Duke of Urbino, where his father was the court painter. His refined and affable manner made him the very model of a Renaissance courtier.

In 1504 Raphael settled in Florence. This was the time when Michelangelo and Leonardo were setting new standards in the world of art. He carefully studied the works of these masters and incorporated many of their techniques into his own style. But there is a unique poetic quality to his paintings, as can be seen in the numerous gentle, sweet-faced Madonnas he created during this period. (Isn't it interesting how an artist's personality is often reflected in the portraits he paints?) The figures of Madonna of the Meadow are classically arranged. As you can see, they form a

Madonna of the Meadow

balanced triangle. The painting has a sense of calm, unity, and harmony – the features so highly valued in ancient classical sculpture.

In 1508 Julius II commissioned Raphael to paint the walls of a suite of chambers in the Vatican Palace. The Pope had in mind a series of frescoes that would reflect the religious and philosophical ideals of the High Renaissance. On the walls of the first room, the Stanza della Segnatura, Raphael painted large frescoes celebrating the four aspects of human accomplishment: theology (*Disputation Over The Sacrament*), philosophy (*School Of Athens*), the arts (*Parnasus*), and law (*Cardinal Virtues And Giving Of The Law*). Each wall in the room has an arch to support the curved ceiling. Raphael ingeniously incorporated this architectural feature into his

School of Athens

pictures. The frescoes combine elements of classical culture and Christian theology, reflecting once again the humanist belief that there can be a harmonious relationship between the two in the search for truth and beauty.

The painting entitled *School Of Athens* established Raphael's reputation. An allegory of secular (non-religious) learning, it portrays Plato and Aristotle surrounded by other famous Greek philosophers as they debate with one another. Plato gestures upwards towards the heavens as the ultimate source of understanding, while Aristotle stretches out his hand, palm down, to indicate the importance of gathering practical knowledge by observing the natural world.

Looking on approvingly from two niches in the walls are statues of the Greek deities, Apollo and Athena. Many of the elegant figures attending the philosophers are portraits of Raphael's contemporaries, including Leonardo da Vinci (who poses as Aristotle), Bramante, and Michelangelo. He even included himself.

The frescoes of the stanze were painted when Michelangelo was just starting work on the ceiling of the Sistine Chapel. Raphael met the older artist at this time, but the gruff Michelangelo disliked the young man immensely and accused him of stealing his ideas. We know that Raphael was influenced by Michelangelo's earlier works, but the main model for his figures was the Apollo

Belvedere in the Vatican Museum. Although Vasari claimed that he sneaked into the chapel at night with architect Bramante, it is most probable that Raphael first viewed the figures on the ceiling in August, 1511, when the scaffolding was temporarily removed to celebrate the feast of the Assumption of the Virgin. So Michelangelo's attacks were unfounded.

Upon the death of Bramante, Pope Leo X placed Raphael in charge of the construction of the new Saint Peter's. (As we know, Michelangelo later took over this command.) There were even rumors that the young artist would be appointed a cardinal. But suddenly he died on Good Friday, 1520, his thirty-seventh birthday. What a terrible loss to the world of art. At Raphael's request he was buried in the Pantheon. His last painting, Transfiguration, unfinished at the time, was displayed over his coffin. Cardinal Bembo wrote the following epitaph:

This is Raphael's tomb, while he lived he made Mother Nature fear to be vanquished by him and, as he died, to die too.

Portrait of Isabella d'Este by Titian

The Gonzaga Court in Mantua

Isabella d'Este (1474-1539). She was born in the duchy of Ferrara and received an outstanding education from the best scholars of the day. She was extremely intelligent and clever, and she easily mastered Greek and Latin, memorized passages from Virgil and Terence, learned to play the lute with skill, perfected the steps of every new dance, embroidered beautifully, and could hold her own in a conversation with the ambassadors who visited her father, Duke Ercole.

Isabella married Francesco Gonzaga of Mantua, just before her sixteenth birthday. Although this was a political alliance, she got along well with

her new husband. Together they reigned over a court that included such creative men as Leonardo da Vinci. The Marquis shared her enjoyment of music, and they commissioned lutes, organs, and clavichords to be made created specifically for their musical gatherings. Isabella wrote thousands of letters to artists, musicians, and government leaders. (She was, in fact, related by birth or marriage to almost every ruler in Italy!) Over 2,000 of her letters survive and tell us much about the thoughts of the leaders of sixteenth century European society.

Isabella was admired for her beauty, good taste, keen mind and political wisdom. Once Francesco was captured during a war with Venice,

Joanna of Aragon by Raphael

The Courtier

Baldassare Castiglione was a diplomat who spent much of his time in the courts of Milan, Mantua, the Vatican and Urbino. Born into a wealthy family residing near Mantua, Castiglione was a contemporary and friend of Raphael, who painted a famous portrait of him. After serving at the court of Francesco Gonzaga, Castiglione took up residence at the court of Urbino, ruled by Duke Guidobaldo da Montrefeltro. Known for its concerts, plays, poetry readings and festivals, the richness and refinement of Urbino's cultural life was overseen by the duke's wife, Elizebetta.

"The Book of the Courtier" is set on four different nights at the court of Urbino. Several people, all drawn from life, have gathered for a discussion of the qualities the ideal courtier should possess. The only two people conspicuously

leaving Isabella in charge of Mantua. Her lively wit and diplomatic discretion enabled her to rule ably, even making allies of former enemies of the Marquis. When her husband returned home, he remarked, "It is our fate to have as a wife a woman who is always ruled by her head." Could he have been envious?

Isabella's study contained so many costly books and great art works it was called *II Paradise*. (She was history's first female collector of great art.) On the ceiling were carved her name and motto: "Neither hope nor fear." (What do you think that means?) When she died (she lived into her sixties) her estate inventories revealed over 1,600 items, including bronze and marble statues, precious stone vases, gems, coins, and medals, cameos, enamels, crystal mirrors, and the paintings she had commissioned.

Baldassare Castiglione by Raphael

Ducal palace at Urbino, setting for The Courtier

Latin. His conversation was witty and refined. (It was considered a cardinal sin to be boring!) He could perform admirably in several sports, particularly wrestling, riding, tennis, and running.

Just as art should conceal the work that goes into its creation, the courtier should be modest and make his achievements seem effortless. Every act should be performed with *sprezzatura* - an unforced ease of accomplishment - and he should discuss his interests knowledgeably without making others feel uncomfortable. In other words, he should do well in everything without seeming to try hard. This quality of effortless superiority would be considered the mark of the gentleman for centuries to come. In fact the word *virtuoso* entered the Italian language in the sixteenth century to describe a towering personality who made an art of his every act.

Castiglione was clearly influenced by the ancient ideal of the responsible citizen with a finely tuned mind and body. To this image of the well-rounded man he added a dash of medieval chivalry: a courtier was encouraged to fall in love with an attractive (and married, thus ineligible) lady of the court. He could reveal his feelings only from a distance, writing love poems and notes praising her beauty.

The Courtier was translated in several languages and became a bestseller throughout much of Europe. As a handbook of proper behavior, it helped to civilize society. However, the book is not without its faults. For example, the courtier is advised never to cheapen himself by mingling with members of the lower classes. Let's not forget that the sophisticated culture of the Italian Renaissance

missing from the proceedings are the author, Castiglione, and the prince himself, Duke Guidobaldo. The mistress of ceremonies, directing the flow of talk, is the duchess.

He was inspired by the elegant men and women of Federico's court to write a book, *The Courtier*, which set forth the standards of gentlemanly conduct (begun 1508, published 1528). Written as a series of after-dinner discussions among the courtiers and ladies of Urbino, it became the standard of taste for western society. Much of what are considered "good manners" in today's world date back to Castiglione's code of behavior.

And what was the ideal courtier? According to Castiglione, he was "well rounded," skillful in many diverse activities. For example, he could play various musical instruments, recite and compose poetry, and dance with grace and elegance. He had a solid knowledge of classics, an understanding of art and sculpture, and the ability to speak several languages, including, of course, Greek and involved only the "upper crust," a small fraction of society, and Castiglione's elitist views will offend modern readers. Furthermore, by emphasizing outward appearances Castiglione actually encouraged the people of the court to indulge in all sorts of evil schemes - even ruthless murders - while hiding behind the mask of impeccable manners.

High Fashion in the Sixteenth Century

We learned earlier about the elegant fashions of the wealthy classes in fifteenth century Italy. By the High Renaissance these had become extremely extravagant and flashy. The courts and major cities of sixteenth century Europe were, in fact, centers of display and ostentation, where the rich tried to outshine one another in their eye-catching finery.

Since medieval times, there had existed a set of official regulations, known as the "sumptuary laws," that specified the types of dress considered appropriate for every social rank. These were originally intended to protect the local weaving industry by limiting the importation of expensive foreign cloth, but they also helped to maintain the social structure. Only the wealthiest members of society were allowed to wear the finest materials. For example, royalty could wear the fur of the ermine, but nobles wore fox. Squirrel or rabbit were acceptable furs for the middle class. The lower classes had to settle for coarsely woven wool, which, of course, was all they could afford anyway. Certain cities limited the number of silk and velvet garments that could be owned by a single person, and in Florence women of the humbler classes were forbidden to make buttons from any material but wood.

Portrait of a Gentleman by Bartolomeo Sauvan-Magnet

Some laws regulated certain styles of dress for reasons of practicality. Remember those long pointed toes that became popular in the fourteenth century? In 1464 an English statute banned any cobbler or leatherworker from making the toe of a courtier's shoe more than two inches long. As a result, the squared-off toe became the rage at the end of the century. Other ordinances in Milan and Venice regulated the low necklines and long trailing skirts among the ladies. However, few people observed these rules. Excess was the norm in high society throughout Europe. Rich French women wore elaborate headdresses that were so high that entrances to rooms and buildings had to be altered for them! Those who could afford it were often tempted to flaunt their leisured status by wearing the most highly impractical and exorbitantly expensive clothing available.

The typical courtier of the sixteenth century strode about like a proud peacock, thanks to the efforts of his personal fashion designer. His detachable puffed sleeves billowed from a short, fitted doublet of satin or velvet and then tapered at the wrist. A stiff fluted collar (called a ruff) often graced his neck. His tight, wool stockings glistened with silver threads. A startling effect could be achieved by wearing stockings of different colors or patterns. Over the doublet he wore a jerkin, usually trimmed with fur and belted at the waist. To complete his costume, the courtier might wear a velvet cap with a feather stuck through its brim, scented leather gloves, golden necklaces, and a sword with an ornate hilt.

A new fashion, known as slashing, had become popular in Germany in the late fifteenth century and then spread throughout Europe. The outer material of a courtier's doublet, sleeve, or hose was cut (slashed), and the contrasting fabrics beneath were pulled through the openings. This produced a very colorful effect. At first the slashings were small, intricate patterns, but in the late sixteenth century they became long, vertical lines. Slashing marks were even imitated with engravings on metal armor.

Slashing originated on the battlefield of Grandson in 1476 when German mercenaries became intrigued by the way the Swiss troops made undergarments from the tattered banners and tents of their enemies - these protruded colorfully through the holes of their own ragged clothing. The popularity of slashing might have begun as a reaction to the sumptuary law forbidding the lower classes to wear clothing of more than one color, but the new look was soon associated with the well-dressed courtier.

In later years, the multi-colored effect of men's clothing was enhanced by a new technique called "bombasting." Garments were thickly stuffed with dyed cotton wool or similar padding. Then the material was slashed and the padding as pulled through. This created a puffier look. Courtiers began to wear short padded breeches that puffed out above the cuffs at mid-thigh. The Spanish ones were called "pumpkin breeches."

The long flowing gowns of the ladies of the court billowed gracefully when they walked. Many of them had long trains, like those of a modern wedding gown. Elaborate head-dresses were made from starched and folded linen, a style originating in northern Europe and quickly spreading to Italy. Some ladies wore a hennin - a high, cone-shaped headdress with a long scarf attached to the peak. This dated from medieval times. When a high forehead became fashionable, the women plucked their eyebrows and shaved their hairlines

Portrait of Giovanna Tornabuoni by Ghirlandaio

to achieve "the look/' Another bizarre fad was clogs -wooden shoes with four-inch heels. These were extremely awkward footwear, although they proved quite useful for keeping long hemlines above the mud of city streets. Eventually, they became so high that a lady had to be supported by her maids when she walked!

Spanish women of the sixteenth century started a new style by wearing rigid corsets made of iron or bone to make their waists seem tiny. Their skirts fit over conical metal frames called farthingales, which further accentuated the narrow appearance of their waists. No wonder these women appear so stiff and somber in their portraits! Before long, all European aristocrats were wearing these terribly uncomfortable contraptions in the hopes of having the perfect hourglass figure. A well-dressed woman also carried a fan, a handkerchief, and a pair of scented gloves.

The brocades and velvets of the apparel of both men and women were often covered with pearls, gold embroidery, and precious stones. Imagine the weight of their clothing, and how hot it must have been in summer! Eager to compete with the courtiers, the wealthy merchants and their wives spent fabulous sums on their own extravagant attire.

The High Renaissance in Venice

Unlike the other Italian cities, Venice was a colonial power whose vast maritime empire stretched eastwards to the island of Cyprus. Its many ports gave Venetian merchants ready access to the points at which spices, silks and dyes from Asia reached the Mediterranean Sea, particularly Alexandria, Egypt. By the dawn of the sixteenth century, Venice also owned a large territory on the Italian mainland, which was known as *Terraferrna*.

The wealthy men who ran the Venetian republic never allowed a single family to seize control, as had happened in Florence and Milan. The apparent ruler, the Doge, was just a figurehead, as we learned earlier. Since there was no court, the artists sought the patronage of the government itself. The leaders of the republic gladly obliged and supported any works that reflected the city's majesty and affluence.

For centuries, Venetian artists had painted on wooden panels made of poplar, oak, or silver fir, but after 1450 a new material - canvas - became the preferred painting surface. This heavy cloth had been used for many years for temporary festival decorations and theatrical scenery. It gradually became popular for other large scale paintings because it could be rolled up and transported easily. Canvas has the added advantage of resisting the ravages of moisture better than wooden panels, and this in itself made it very popular in the damp city of Venice. (Relatively few Venetian artists considered painting a fresco, since this process requires a dry environment.) Canvas proved to be the ideal surface for oil paint. Venetian artists won great praise for their oil paintings. Unlike the artists of Florence and Rome, who were noted for their skillful application of the rules of perspective and their realistic (although idealized) rendering of the human body, the Venetians became famous for their use of lighting to add dimension and drama and their bright colors.

Giovanni Bellini (1430-1516) was the first Venetian artist to master the use of oils. He was trained by his father, Jacopo, a fine painter in his own right, and produced a number of vivid portraits and richly glowing altarpieces. Giovanni had a knack for transforming the mundane routines of everyday life into special, meditative moments. He broke from the tradition of Byzantine art (until now most Venetians were directly influenced by the nearby Byzantines) by placing his figures in natural positions and surrounding them with realistic landscapes. But it is the warmth of his colors and the intricacy of detail achieved by the slow-drying oil paints that make his works memorable. Bellini was appointed the official painter of the Venetian republic in 1483 and is credited with establishing Venice as an artistic center on a level with Florence and Rome.

One of Bellini's most admired paintings is *The Ecstasy of Saint Francis*. It depicts the twelfth century saint having a religious ecstasy, his face lifted to the heavens. Look at all the wonderful details in this scene. Although it is dawn, the scene is filled with light. Notice there are two sources of light – one in the distant sky, the other coming directly from the left. This second source of light is said to be coming from the Holy Spirit.

In 1527 Rome was sacked by a Spanish army. (We'll find out why in the next chapter.) This vicious attack caused Roman artists and scholars to flee to other cities. Doge Andrea Gritti enticed many of them to come to Venice. The contributions of these exiles would help to make Venice a dynamic cultural center celebrated not only for its oil paintings but for its architecture, music, and craftsmanship.

Titian

Tiziano Vecellio (1488-1576), known as Titian, was the dominant painter of the Venetian Renaissance. He was a prolific artist - an extraordinary 400 of his paintings have survived. Born in the Alps, Titian went to Venice as a young man to study painting and worked there throughout most of his long life. (He lived to be ninety.) In the early years, he studied with Giovanni Bellini, who allegedly remarked that the boy drew his figures so fast that he would "never succeed as a painter." It was another artist, Giorgione, who taught him a bold brush technique and how to apply a glaze to make a painting appear bright and shimmery. Titian so totally mastered the techniques of Giorgione that modern authorities are unsure

Ecstasy of Saint Francis

whether certain works of the period were a collaboration of the two artists or were done by one or the other - and if so, which one!

Woman with a Mirror

In 1516 Titian became the official painter of the Venetian Republic, but this did not prevent him from accepting commissions from other Italian cities. In 1518 he completed the large altarpiece painting, *The Assumption Of The Virgin*. By applying thick layers of individual brushstrokes in pure colors, chiefly red, white, yellow, and black, he created the illusion of well-rounded figures whose skin seems to glow with incandescent light. In painting *Madonna With Saints*, Titian disregarded the traditional rules of composition, placing Mary and the child to the side of the main focus. Compared to the classical works we have studied, this one appears lopsided and unbalanced, but Titian relied upon his mastery of color and brushstroke to bring everything together. Titian's

Woman with a Mirror has beautiful reddish hair that is so typical of the artist's paintings that women with red hair came to be referred to as Titian-like. She actually is regarding herself by the use of two mirrors: Titian was very interested in the interplay of image and reflection. The two mirrors make it possible for us to see the woman from different sides, just like a statue.

Pietro Aretino was a writer and courtier who arrived in Venice in 1527. He became Titian's friend and publicity agent. Aretino distributed pamphlets about the artist's talent and arranged for his introduction to Holy Roman Emperor Charles V, who commissioned Titian to paint his portrait. The full-length figure he produced exudes such elegance that Charles immediately appointed him court painter and even knighted him. According to legend, the Emperor once did the artist the honor of picking up a brush he had dropped. The image of a powerful ruler humbling himself before a painter indicates how greatly the prestige of the artist had grown since the fourteenth century. Titian and Charles developed a close relationship

Ecce Homo

that lasted for years, and the Emperor's portrait made full-length paintings fashionable throughout Europe.

Widely sought after by kings, princes, and popes, Titian was one of the few painters of his time to acquire a fortune through his art. He was a rapid worker, which explains why he completed so many paintings. Although he was well known for his religious, mythological, and historical paintings, his fame rests upon his portraits. He had a talent for penetrating the personality of the sitter and conveying it with dignity and vitality. His paintings have a sensual quality about them because of his ability to depict so convincingly the textures of velvet, fur, flesh, jewels, and metal.

When he visited Rome in 1543 to paint a portrait of Pope Paul III, Titian met Michelangelo. The older artist complemented him on his "lively manner" of painting, but he added that it was "a pity good design was not taught in Venice." And yet, design, in the sense Michelangelo used the word, became less important to Titian as he relied more upon the effects of color and brushstroke to create an emotional impact. In his later masterpiece, *Ecce Homo*, the figure emerges from the semidarkness and shimmers with light that seems to radiate from within. Vasari, who visited the artist in his Venetian workshop in 1566, remarked that Titian "walks in step with nature: hence each one of his figures is alive and in motion, with flesh that quivers."

Palladio

Architectural design in the later years of the sixteenth century was dominated by Andrea di Pietro della Gondola, known as Palladio. Trained as a stonemason, he became the protégé of humanist scholar and amateur architect, Count Giangiorgio Trissino. Trissino taught him Latin and encouraged his interest in ancient art and architecture. He nicknamed him Palladio after the mythological patron goddess of the arts, Pallas Athena. (Some historians claim he was named after the fourth-century Roman writer Palladius. Take your pick!) The two men traveled together to Rome on three occasions. Each time Palladio studied and carefully sketched many of the ancient ruins. He

the Villa Rotunda

San Giorgio Maggiore, Venice

The use of symmetrical wings projecting from the sides of a central structure were to become hallmarks of his style. He introduced the temple front (tall pillars topped by a triangular pediment) to the design of villas and palazzos. The pediment was often decorated with the family's coat of arms. He also created the Palladian window: an arched window consisting of three panels, the middle one higher than the other two.

His most famous domestic dwelling, the Villa Rotunda near Vicenza, is a model of classical symmetry. Viewed from above it is a perfect square, with four smaller squares (porches coming off of each side. The villa is crowned with a dome, clearly inspired by the Pantheon in Rome. Palladio's use of a central dome on a villa was a bold innovation, but it was so well received that it led to a long tradition of domed country homes. His elegant private palaces and majestic public buildings made Venice's Grand Canal the most beautiful thoroughfare in Europe.

published his drawings in a guidebook on the antiquities of classical Rome. But what he really wanted to do was design his own buildings, and he soon got his chance.

Like Vasari, he incorporated many of the features of the ancient structures, such as columns, pilasters, and loggias (colonnades) into his designs of churches, civic buildings, villas, and palazzos.

Palladio devoted more than twenty years to the preparation of his famous treatise, *Four Books Of Architecture*. This massive work explains the principles of Vitruvius and Alberti in a manner that is easy to understand. It is filled with plans, elevations, and decorative schemes for his own buildings, a clever marketing strategy that helped to promote his designs throughout Europe. Palladio created the first international style of architecture since the Gothic structures of the Middle Ages. It is known today as neoclassicism ("new classicism"). President (and architect) Thomas Jefferson owned a copy of his treatise and consulted it frequently when he designed his own Virginia home, *Monticello*, as well as the buildings of the University of Virginia.

Neo-classical building at the University of Virginia

From Harmony to Distortion

The artists of the High Renaissance certainly scaled the heights of excellence. How could the generations that came after them hope to compete with such masterpieces? What was there left to accomplish? The response of many younger artists was to adopt a completely different approach to art. They are known as Mannerists. The term "Mannerism" comes from the Italian word *maniera*. During the sixteenth century *maniera* referred to playfulness in art. The object was to be inventive, not as a means of depicting nature, but as an end in itself.

The Mannerists often exaggerated features of Renaissance art, just for fun. For example, where Michelangelo had drawn and sculpted many nudes in twisted or contorted positions to express their inner anguish, the new generation of artists filled biblical scenes with hordes of energetic, twisting, muscle-bound figures! Some artists played with obscure symbolism (were they teasing the intellectual art lovers?), while others sought to draw attention to their works by totally disregarding the balance and symmetry of classical works and filling their canvases with bizarre and unnatural objects. One critic remarked that Mannerists seemed to find beauty in things that were deformed and sought to please by giving displeasure.

The Madonna With The Long Neck by Parmigianino (begun in 1532) is an excellent example of Mannerism. The figures have strangely elongated bodies. The Virgin has the long graceful neck of a swan, which contrasts with her massive legs. Her odd physique resembles the metal jug which is (inexplicably) being carried by a young man. She holds an over-sized squirming body, who seems to be falling out of her lap. A prophet appears in the distance, but he is so radically reduced in size that he looks like an elf at the Madonna's feet! And rather than distribute the figures in an orderly and balanced manner, Parmigianino has crammed a group of angels into one small corner of the painting.

Benvenuto Cellini (1500-71) was a Florentine goldsmith and sculptor. His *Autobiography* (inspired by Vasari's LIVES) gives us a fascinating account of the life of an artist in the later sixteenth century. This is not to say that Cellini was typical. He was a scoundrel, who traveled from court to court seeking his fortune and escaping punishment for his petty crimes. But in the process he created some beautiful objects - jewelry, seals, and metalwork - for nobles, popes, and sovereigns.

One of the few pieces of Cellini to survive until our times is an elaborate gold and enamel saltcellar on an ebony base, which he presented to Francis I of France in 1543. It is a typically Mannerist piece

Madonna with the Long Neck

of art, a "tour de force" of inventiveness and caprice. Two nude figures, representing the earth and the sea, recline in rather awkward positions. The earth figure resembles Aphrodite, the Greek goddess of love and beauty, while the other figure appears to be Poseidon, Greek god of the sea. She sits beside a disproportionately small Greek temple, which holds the pepper, while he carries an under-sized but finely wrought ship, which contains the salt. Can you imagine such an elaborate "salt and pepper set" gracing our modern tables? Cellini wrote in his book that when he was carrying the gold for the saltcellar to his workshop he was attacked by four thieves, all of whom he defeated single-handedly. (He was also somewhat of a braggart!)

Cellini's saltcellar

In 1545 Cellini was accused of embezzling precious metals and gemstones. So he fled from France back to Florence, where he persuaded Duke Cosimo I (de Medici) to commission a bronze statue of Perseus and Medusa. The attractive Greek hero Perseus stands triumphantly atop the gruesome bleeding trunk of the monster Medusa, holding her severed head in his hand. His eyes

are averted, since a glance at her eyes will turn him to stone. Today you can see the statue in the loggia beside the Piazza della Signoria in Florence. Although Cellini's Perseus was closer to nature than the art of most Mannerists, Michelangelo dismissed the artist as "a maker of snuffbox ornaments!"

Perseus and Medusa

The greatest painter of the late sixteenth century was Venetian artist Jacopo Robusti, known as Tintoretto (1518-1594). His nickname means "little dyer," a reference to his father's trade as a dyer (*tintore*). He was a pupil of Titian, from whom he learned much about the use of color, brushstroke, and the effects of chiaroscuro. Tintoretto often made wax and clay models and set them in a box with a candle in order to experiment with different lighting effects. He covered his vast canvases with dramatic scenes. Unlike the classical paintings, his works seem disorderly and confusing - so much is happening at once. In *Saint Mark Working Miracles*, the intensity of the action is increased by the abrupt contrast of light and darkness. Saint Mark, the patron saint of Venice, stands with his hand raised, performing such miracles as raising a man from the dead and restoring a blind man's sight. Meanwhile, tomb robbers are busily stealing bodies from their tombs! How eccentric this work seems when compared with one of the balanced and refined paintings of Raphael or Leonardo!

Although Mannerism began in Italy, it eventually spread throughout much of the rest of Europe. It would later evolve into the Baroque style of the seventeenth century.

Review questions

1. According to Vasari, what were the three stages of the rebirth of art?

2. What was the advantage of oil paint over tempera?

3. Describe, in detail, Leonardo's *Mona Lisa*.

4. What was so special about Pope Nicholas V?

5. What were some of the original statues in the papal collection of antique sculpture?

6. Who was Bramante?

7. In what ways did Pope Leo X reflect the interests of his father, Lorenzo the Magnificent?

8. What did Michelangelo consider himself? (A painter or a sculptor or both?)

9. Describe Michelangelo's *Pieta*.

10. What did Michelangelo's statue of David symbolize?

11. What is the connection between Brunelleschi's dome in Florence and Michelangelo's dome in Rome?

12. Describe the School of Athens.

13. Describe the ideal courtier.

14. How did Venetian art differ from Florentine art?

15. What are the main characteristics of the paintings of Titian?

16. Describe Palladio's style of architecture.

17. What is Mannerism?

18. How did mannerist art differ from classical art?

Further Thoughts

1. Leonardo da Vinci was inspired by the many-volumed work by Roman architect Vitruvius to draw the ideal male figure, known as Vitruvian Man, in his notebook. Vitruvius believed the circle and square to be perfect shapes, and described how the body of a human being could fit perfectly within those shapes. Leonardo drew a man in a spread-eagled position (arms up legs apart) to show that he fit into perfect circle. Then, in the same drawing, he showed him with his feet together and arms outstretched, fitting easily into a perfect square. This view of measuring the world in terms of man is an ancient one (a Greek philosopher once wrote, "Man is the measure of all things) and was central to humanist philosophy.

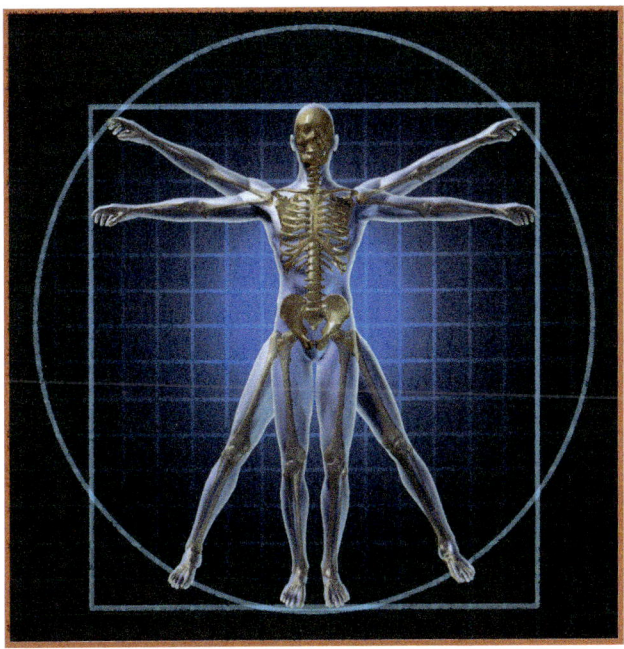

Vitruvian Man

2. As a young art student, Michelangelo once was given the head of a statue to copy. He

did such a good job that when he returned the copy to the owner in place of the original (having buried it for a time in a vineyard to make it seem older), the man didn't notice any difference. The truth only came out when Michelangelo was overheard telling a friend about what he had done. Later, when he was living in Lorenzo's villa, Michelangelo's statue of a sleeping Cupid was successfully sold by a dealer as a genuine work of antiquity. It was later purchased by Isabella d'Este, the famed art patroness of the court of Mantua.

3.   Today Saint Peter's is protected by the Swiss Guards. Their costumes were designed by Michelangelo and Raphael. They are Swiss because they are recruited among Swiss Catholics. Vatican City is an independent country, the smallest in the world.

4.   Intellectually gifted men, who in modern times might turn to science or math, were drawn during the Renaissance to art and architecture. They were intrigued by the complex harmonies that could be achieved by following the strict rules of linear perspective.

A Swiss Guard

5.   When he began to sculpt Michelangelo envisioned the presence of a statue within the stone that needed to be set free. So, in a manner of speaking, he considered himself a liberator rather than a creator. Some of his late statues of bound slaves seem as if they are indeed struggling to free themselves from their stone prisons.

6.   Vasari was proud of the fact that he could paint very quickly. When he bragged to Michelangelo about how he had completed the Great Hall in the Chancellor's Palace in Rome in 100 days, the great artist sniffed, "That's obvious."

7.   Vittoria Colonna (1490-1547) was betrothed at the age of four and married at nineteen to Ferdinando d'Avalos, Marquis of Pescara. She deeply loved her husband (another exception to the rule), and after his untimely death she retired to a convent. Eventually, she settled in Rome. Like Isabella d'Este, she had many famous literary friends and correspondents, including Castiglione and Michelangelo (who addressed a number of poems and letters to her). Vittoria was a renowned poet in her own right. Her collection of Petrarchan sonnets in rime were written, she said, to relieve the pain of her grieving for Ferdinando.

8.   Beatrice del Sera (1515-86) became a nun because she had no dowry. She was so unhappy about being placed in the convent against her will that she focused her energies into the writing of morality plays. *Love Of Virtue* is a particularly moving protest against the conventional imprisonment of women by men. Indeed, weren't most women prisoners in one way or another? One character complains that women are not born for happiness but to serve others. The play is filled with symbolic images of rocks, walls, and towers, all of which confined most women born in those difficult times against their wills.

Projects

1. Why do you suppose Leonardo wrote his notebooks in reverse? Try some mirror writing, just for fun. Then write a paragraph expressing your opinions about why Leonardo wrote in this unusual way.

2. Read a few of the sonnets of Michelangelo.

3. Make a timeline of the eighty-eight years of Michelangelo's life, noting major political events as well as his own artistic accomplishments.

4. The tools of the sculptor have changed very little since early times. They consist of hammers and pointed chisels. Find out how these tools are used to turn a block of stone into a figure. Make a poster to illustrate the process.

5. Think about the personalities and interests of Leonardo, Michelangelo, and Raphael. Then write a short skit about them. Pretend that they are middle school kids living in today's world. Have them argue about something, such as who will do the decorations for school play. This can be a comedy or a serious drama.

6. Leonardo once wrote, "Impatience, the mother of stupidity, praises brevity." What does this mean? How does the quote relate to the lifetime accomplishments of Leonardo? Can you think of an example from your daily experiences to which the quote aptly applies?

7. Leonardo once described the eye as the window of the soul. What did he mean by that? Write a paragraph explaining your views. Give examples.

8. El Greco (Domenikos Theotokopoulos) of Crete visited Venice and was drawn to the paintings of Tintoretto. He later settled in Toledo, Spain, and produced paintings even more startling and unorthodox than those of the Venetian painter. Find out more about him.

9. Obtain a copy of Cellini's *Autobiography* and read several chapters.

10. Aristotle wrote that artists should "paint people better than they are." Choose three Renaissance artists and explain how they followed the Greek philosopher's advice.

School of athens

CHAPTER 6

THE ITALIAN WARS

Do you remember reading about the Peace of Lodi, the mutual non-aggression pact among the five major powers of Italy (Venice, Milan, Florence, Naples, and the Papal Lands)? It had been signed in 1454. Until the death of Lorenzo the Magnificent in 1492, the peace had been maintained. But then new conflicts arose that would lead to great turmoil throughout much of Italy.

A Fight for Power

The problems began in Milan in 1480, when Francesco Sforza's second son, Ludovico, gained control of the government. His older brother had just died, so he proclaimed himself regent for his seven-year-old nephew. Ludovico was known as *Il Moro* (the Moor) because of his dark complexion. He was an able ruler and a well-educated patron of the arts. He married Beatrice d'Este of Mantua (the sister of Isabella, Marquise of Urbino) and presided over an elegant court. It was Ludovico who brought Leonardo da Vinci to Milan and commissioned The Last Supper, among other famous works of art.

When Ludovico's nephew died (under mysterious circumstances), he named himself Duke of Milan. But there was another nephew who was the legitimate heir to this title, and he sought the support of his grandfather, the powerful King Alfonzo of Naples. Now Ludovico was really in a fix. So, to secure his position and preoccupy King Alfonzo, he encouraged Charles VIII of France to claim his ancient rights to southern Italy. (Charles, who succeeded Louis XI, was related to the ruling family in Naples through his great grandfather.) Charles marched his troops through

Italy in 1494 and set into motion the Italian Wars, a long series of battles to gain power and territory, marked by multiple alliances, counter-alliances, and betrayals. The wars would drag on for over half a century.

Florence at this point was led by Piero de Medici. When Charles led his French troops to the city, Piero immediately surrendered. (As we learned in Chapter 4, the Florentines booted out Piero for betraying them.) Then Charles marched south, drove off Alfonzo, and had himself crowned King of Naples. When he returned to France, he left his army garrisoned in Italy.

The presence of the French soldiers was an unbearable affront to the Italians, and it prompted the five signers of the Treaty of Lodi (including Milan) to look for another foreign ally. They appealed to King Ferdinand of Aragon, who obligingly sent his army down the Italian peninsula to surround the French soldiers. After some terrible fighting, those French who survived fled home. But now there were Spanish soldiers

The Sforza castle in Milan

garrisoned in Italy! The Italians were no better off than they were before.

But let's get back to Milan, where the problems began. In 1500 Louis XII of France (who succeeded Charles VIII) invaded Ludovico's city. (He had inherited a claim to Milan through his grandfather.) The city fell to the French. Louis continued on to Naples but was driven back by the Spanish army.

So now the French army controlled parts of northern Italy from a base in Milan, while the Spanish remained firmly entrenched in the south. As for Ludovico, he was captured by the French. He spent his last days in an underground dungeon in the French castle of Loches.

Cesare Borgia

Cesare Borgia, the son of Pope Alexander VI, played a vital role in the politics of central Italy at this time. He was a ruthless and brutal man, one of the great villains of history, although he looked more like a hero. He was quite handsome, with big shoulders, a slim waist, long, thick hair, and blazing blue eyes. Cesare was made a cardinal by his father in 1493, but he renounced his career with the Church five years later for a more active military life. His father made him the leader of the Papal army, which he led against the rebelling Papal States. He was supported in his military campaign by Louis XII of France, who granted him the title of Duke of Valentinois. (By allying with Cesare, Louis cleverly extended the French influence into central Italy.)

Now known to the local citizens as *Il Valentino*, he used treason, murder, and intrigue to crush the noble families that were opposing the Pope. He strangled and tortured many a foe, and even knifed a suspected papal official, who had run to

Cesare Borgia by Giovanni di Lutero

Alexander for refuge and was cowering in fear under the Pope's mantle!

In 1502 he swept down on Urbino and forced the rulers to flee. He appropriated the priceless art collection of Isabella d'Este, much of which he sold to pay his troops. But Cesare had made many enemies, and several of his leading condottiere conspired against him. He called his loyal generals to his side and waited for the alliance of his enemies to collapse, which it did. Cesare then summoned the defeated condottiere, offering them a reconciliation. But when they arrived, he had them arrested. They were later executed.

The death of Alexander signaled the end of Cesare's political career. Although the new pope, Pius III, supported him, he soon died and was succeeded by Julius II, a sworn enemy of the Borgias. Cesare was forced to give up his strongholds, and when it became clear that his life was in danger, he fled to Naples, and then to Spain. He was imprisoned by Ferdinand of Spain but escaped to Navarre. Cesare was finally killed in 1507 at the siege of Viana, fighting for his brother-in-law, the King of Navarre.

Meanwhile, the Italian Wars intensified. Attention was turned to Venice, whose territory was rapidly expanding across northern Italy. Emperor Maximilian joined Pope Julius, King Louis XII, and King Ferdinand in the League of Cambrai (1508), an alliance against Venice. The League conquered all of Venice's mainland possessions. But quarrels over dividing up the spoils led to the formation of a new alliance - this time between Julius, Maximilian and Ferdinand. This was known as the Holy League. King Louis was now the loser, and his French army was forced out of Milan.

Machiavelli

All of the political maneuverings of Italian and foreign leaders were viewed with great interest by Niccolo Machiavelli (1469-1527), an Italian historian, politician, diplomat, philosopher, humanist, and writer. He lived in Florence during the turbulent times of the Italian Wars. After the fall of Savonarola in 1498, Florence had created a new republican government. Machiavelli served for many years as an official in the republic, with major responsibilities in diplomatic and military affairs. His high status enabled him to make numerous diplomatic missions, where he met many of the most powerful political figures of the time, including Louis XII, Maximilian I, Pope Julius, and even Cesare Borgia. Machiavelli carefully observed the political intrigues taking place on every front. He saw how the city-states tried to protect themselves by playing off the larger powers against one another and by hiring armies

of mercenaries, which they then had difficulty controlling.

In 1512, the Medici returned to Florence. But things would never be the same as they were in the days of Lorenzo. The Medici established a dynasty of dukes, who no longer made any effort to hide the fact that they ruled the city. The old spirit of optimism and experimentation that had nurtured Florence's golden age was gone. Nor did things go well for Machiavelli. The Medici unfairly accused him of opposing them and ordered him imprisoned and even tortured.

When he was released a year later, Machiavelli returned to his country estate on the outskirts of Florence. There he spent most of his days socializing with his friends and former political colleagues, but each evening he retired to his study - dressed in the elegant garments he had once worn so proudly as a public official - to work on his writings. He was particularly interested in analyzing the egotistical ways of man and the ruthless realities of political power. He studied the writings of the ancients to learn how they coped with the crises of their era, hoping that he could apply their solutions to the problems of his own age. As it turned out, he came to very different conclusions about the responsibilities of leadership than they had.

After much thought and study, Machiavelli wrote *The Prince*, a practical guide to running a government. It would become a landmark in political theory. The book was dedicated to Lorenzo the Magnificent's grandson Lorenzo, the Duke of Urbino), whom he addressed as the Prince. The book was intended to advise the young man how to cope in the cut-throat world of politics.

Machiavelli's bitter experiences had convinced him that morality and government were two separate things, and in *The Prince* he discussed the sources of power without regard for their

Statue of Machiavelli

ethical or moral content. In fact, Cesare Borgia, known for his cruelty and ruthless tactics, was a model for the book. Machiavelli admired the way Cesare welcomed his enemies as friends and then coldheartedly strangled them! Like Il Valentino, the young Duke was advised, it was the cleverest deceiver who won the game.

Machiavelli advises the Duke to accept people as they are. Why waste time worrying about what they ought to be? So what are people really like? According to the author, they are ungrateful, undependable, false, and greedy. And a wise ruler should appeal to their selfish motives. Machiavelli glorified the qualities of the lion (force) and the fox (slyness). A prince must be powerful and crafty; lies and deceit are totally acceptable if they accomplish a goal. The end justifies the means. Why be hampered by such noble values as honesty, justice, or honor? What works is good, what doesn't isn't. Above all, a prince's

authority must be absolute and unquestioned. "It is better to be feared than loved," Machiavelli wrote, "if you cannot be both." The treatise concludes with a plea for the rescue of Italy from the "barbarian forces" currently occupying it, namely the French and imperial armies.

The Prince was not published until after the death of Machiavelli in 1532. As you might expect, it immediately drew tirades of criticism. Its fundamental concepts are very different from the political theories of Aristotle, who considered politics a branch of ethics (rules of conduct based upon principles of right and wrong). Most Italians, despite the obvious corruption of their own society, seemed to believe that government should be run in a fair and judicial manner. But didn't the humanists encourage everyone to open their eyes and minds to the real world? Artists like Giotto and Leonardo da Vinci tried to show how men really look. Machiavelli wanted to show how men really think. Because he lived at a time of violence, crime, and corruption, he simply documented what he saw going on around him.

The Prince gained enormous notoriety and a wide readership because Machiavelli seemed to be endorsing behavior usually considered evil and immoral. Machiavelli's name became a byword for godlessness, cynicism, and treachery. Even today, "machiavellian" is a pejorative adjective applied to someone who does what is most practical, even if it is not ethical. Many scholars view *The Prince* as a precursor of state crimes in the modern world. And yet, *The Prince* was closely studied by many European rulers, and it is considered a classic treatise by political theorists in our own times. In fact, Machiavelli is viewed as the founder of modern political science, and, more specifically, of political ethics.

The End of the Italian Wars

In 1515 the new French king, Francis I, led an army across the Alps and reconquered Milan. Soon afterwards, both Ferdinand and Maximilian died, and Charles V became Holy Roman Emperor. So now Francis and Charles were the major players in the Italian Wars. In 1525 Charles defeated the French army at Pavia in northern Italy, capturing Francis himself and sending him to a prison in Spain. The French king was released the next year on the condition that he surrender all the Italian territory he had claimed. But France was not yet out of the picture.

The new pope, Clement VII, was worried about the political ambitions of Charles, so he allied himself with Francis, as well as Henry VIII of England and the cities of Florence and Venice, in the League of Cognac in 1526. In response, Charles sent an army to Italy. It conquered Milan and then marched on Rome in 1527, hoping to convince the Pope to quit the League. But the army commander was killed soon after their successful assault of the city and discipline completely broke down. The soldiers savagely sacked Rome for a week, murdering priests and looting churches and cathedrals. Clement took refuge in the strongly fortified Castel San Angelo before surrendering. Charles later released the Pope for a huge ransom and withdrew his men from Rome. He had proven his might and brought the Pope under his (temporary) control, but the sack of Rome shocked the Christian world. Was nothing sacred during these war-ridden times?

Francis continued to meddle in Italian affairs until political setbacks forced him to sign the Treaty of Cateau-Cambresis in 1559, by which he renounced all claims in Italy. That was the end of French involvement in Italy. With the exception of Venice and the Papal Lands, the proud and independent Italian city-states were now in the hands of the Spanish Habsburgs. They would control much of Italy until the early eighteenth century.

The Legacy of the Italian Renaissance

The political disruption of the Italian Wars had brought the Italian Renaissance to an end. The legacy of the Italian Renaissance is a rich one, indeed. That exciting era of innovation in politics, society, and culture marks the transition between medieval and early modern Europe. Breaking away from the strangle hold of the Church, while still honoring the basic beliefs and biblical traditions, insightful men and women of the Renaissance took their cue from humanists like Petrarch. They rediscovered the brilliant culture of the classical past, studied it, and applied its values to their own society.

Writers expressed themselves in their own language rather than Latin. Philosophers came up with new concepts that linked Greek mythology with Christian dogma. Merchants, taking advantage of a flourishing economy, became so wealthy they could use much of their income to become patrons of the arts. Artists created paintings and statues that reflected the reality of this world, not the spirituality of the heavenly realm. Architects applied the symmetry and balance of classical buildings to their own designs. Leonardo da Vinci became fascinated by so many fields of endeavor – from scientific inquiry and invention of new devices to painting with oils – that he often left one project to begin another. He became the quintessential Renaissance Man. Castiglione marveled at the glittering court of Urbino and laid out his vision of the ideal gentleman and lady, while Machiavelli described the way society actually functioned amid corruption and vice.

By the mid-sixteenth, the center of power and influence had been transferred from Italy to the most prosperous states in northern Europe – Spain, France, the Low Countries, Germany, and England. Apart from warfare, economics played an important role in this change. No longer was the Mediterranean Europe's most important trade route. In 1498, Vasco da Gama reached India, and from that date the primary route of goods from the Far East was through such Atlantic ports as Lisbon, Seville, Nantes, Antwerp, and London. These cities became very wealthy, while Italy's economy declined.

As Italy declined in political and economic influence, the ideas and ideals of the Renaissance endured and spread into other parts of Europe. Such hallmarks of the Italian Renaissance as a belief in the potential of mankind, a curiosity about all manner of things, and a striving to bring science and philosophy into the arts were embraced by thinkers, artists, and leaders in the cities to the north. At the same time, the Mannerist style of painting that had evolved in Italy became popular in France and the Netherlands. This great interest in the rich culture of the Italian Renaissance led to a new explosion of innovation and creativity beyond Italy's borders – we know it as the Northern Renaissance.

Review Questions

1. What started the Italian Wars?
2. What good things did Ludovico Sforza do for Milan?
3. What caused Cesare Borgia to fall from power?
4. Describe Machiavelli's political philosophy.
5. What is the importance of Machiavelli today?
6. What major European powers fought in Italy during the Italian Wars?
7. What was the outcome of the Italian Wars?
8. What is the Northern Renaissance?

Further Thoughts

1. Lucrezia Borgia (1480-1519), the daughter of Pope Alexander VI, married three European rulers before she was twenty-two. Her father annulled the first marriage to Giovanni Sforza (because he, the Pope, quarreled with his Milanese family) and ordered the murder of the second husband (because he was a political foe). When Alexander died and her brother (Cesare) was killed in battle, a mourning Lucrezia donned a hairshirt (a garment of scratchy cloth worn next to the skin as a form of penance). She engaged in charity works and pawned her jewels to give alms to the poor. Eventually, however, she re-entered high society. Her third marriage, to Alfonso d'Este, Duke of Ferrara (and brother of Isabella), was a happy one. She devoted the early years of this marriage to charitable works and the education of her seven children. Later, she made the court of Ferrara a brilliant center for artists, poets, and scholars. She was also quite a fashion plate. Her huge wardrobe included fifty gowns, twenty hats, thirty-three pairs of shoes, sixty pairs of slippers, and twenty mantles.

2. When the Medici returned to Florence, they suspected Machiavelli of plotting against them. They wanted to know more about what he had done (what they thought he had done), so once he was imprisoned they subjected him to the "strappado": Hands tied behind his back, he was strung to the ceiling and repeatedly plunged to the floor. The torture was to stop when he began talking. But Machiavelli later prided himself on not uttering a word.

Projects

1. Consult the Internet to learn more about the Italian Wars. Then make a timeline of the major battles and alliances.

2. Here are some quotes from *The Prince*. Explain in your own words what they mean.

- Entrepreneurs are simply those who understand that there is little difference between obstacle and opportunity and are able to turn both to their advantage.

- The more sand has escaped from the hourglass of our life, the clearer we should see through it.

- If an injury is to be done to a man, it should be so severe that vengeance need not be feared.

- Entrepreneurs are simply those who understand that there is little difference between obstacle and opportunity and are able to turn both to their advantage.

- Hatred is gained as much by good works as by evil.

- It is double pleasure to deceive the deceiver.

3. Think about what you've learned in this book about the Italian Renaissance. Then choose a specific area: literature, art, architecture, or politics. Write a short paper about how certain aspects of Renaissance culture in the area you've chosen can be seen in our modern society.

4. Select a man or woman who contributed a great deal to the culture of the Italian Renaissance. Using the Internet or your library, write a report about him or her.

INDEX

Alberti 73-74

architecture 9, 10, 59-60, 61-62, 68-72, 74, 92-93, 109-110

banking 57-58

Bellini, Giovanni 106-107

Boccaccio 22-23

Borgia, Cesare 91, 118-119, 120

Borgia, Lucrezia 91, 122

Botticelli 79-80

Bramante 92-93

Brunelleschi 67-72

Byzantine art 28-29

Castiglione, Baldassare 102-103

Cellini, Benvenuto 11-112

Cimabue 33-34

cuisine 75-76

D'Este, Isabella 101-102, 117

da Feltra, Vittorino 50-51

da Montefeltro, Federico 51-52

Dante 18-21, 23, 25

de Medici, Cosimo 58-62

de Medici, Lorenzo 76-79, 94

Doctrines of the Catholic Church 12

Donatello 65-67

education 14-15, 49-51, 78-79, 101

fashions 62-64, 103-106

Florence 45-49

Fra Angelico 61-62

fresco 31-33, 100

Giotto 34-36

Gonzaga, Francesco 101

Gothic art 27

Gozzoli, Benozzo 60-61

humanism 15-16, 75, 121

Julius II, Pope 91-93, 96, 99

Leo X, Pope 81, 93-94

Leonardo 6, 85-90, 113, 117

Machiavelli 119-120

Mannerism 110-112

Mantua 49, 56, 101-10?

manuscripts 11, 13, 89, 90

Masaccio 72-73

Michelangelo 5, 93-99, 113, 114

Middle Ages 11-14

Milan 43-44, 117-118

Naples 45

Nicholas V, Pope 90-91

Palladio 109-110

Papal States 44-45

Peace of Lodi 49, 117

Petrarch 7, 21-22, 25

Pisano 29-31

Platonic Academy 60, 76

Raphael 99-101

Savonarolo 80-82

Sforza, Francesco 43-44, 60

Sforza, Ludovico 87, 117

Tintoretto 112

Titian 107-109

trade 11, 39, 45-46, 48

Treaty of Cateau-Cambresis 121

Urbino 51-52

Vasari, Giogio 85

Venice 41-43, 106-107

women 53-54, 101-102, 105-106, 114

Holger W. Körtge

Populäre Literatur in Kenia: Der Neue David Maillu - "Benni Kamba 009" als afrikanischer Agenten-Held

GRIN Verlag

Populäre Literatur in Kenia: Der Neue David Maillu — *Benni Kamba 009* als afrikanischer Agenten-Held

Hausarbeit zum Seminar

Populäre afrikanische Literaturen

im Wintersemester 06/07

Institut für Ethnologie und Afrikastudien

Johannes Gutenberg Universität Mainz

vorgelegt von

Holger W. Körtge

Inhaltsverzeichnis

1. Einführung 3

    1.1   Einleitung 3

    1.2   David Maillu 3

2. Benni Kamba 009 5

    2.1   Der Held 5

    2.2   Die Handlung 6

    2.2.1   Benni Kamba 009 in The Equatorial Assignment 6

    2.2.2   Benni Kamba 009 in Operation DXT 6

3. Der neue David Maillu 7

4. Benni Kamba 009 als afrikanischer Agent – Kopie oder Innovation? 10

5. Zusammenfassung 15

6. Literatur 16

1. Einführung

1.1   Einleitung

David Maillu ist einer der erfolgreichsten Autoren Kenias, und der produktivste Schriftsteller in Afrika, wenn man bedenkt, dass über die Hälfte seiner Werke noch gar nicht publiziert sind. Seit seiner ersten Verlagsgründung hat man ihm jedoch immer wieder Steine in den Weg gelegt. Man warf ihm vor, obszöne, pornographische Literatur zu schreiben[1], und seine Bücher wurden in Tansania verboten. Andere haben seinen Erfolg allein der detaillierten Darstellung von Sexualität zugeschrieben.

Im folgenden möchte ich diese Ansicht widerlegen und anhand seiner in den 1980er Jahren veröffentlichten Romane Benni Kamba 009 zeigen, dass David Maillu ein bedeutender Schriftsteller ist, der ein ungeheuer kreatives Potential besitzt, und dass sein schlechter Ruf nur durch seine wenigen Werke der 1970er entstanden ist.

Darüber hinaus möchte ich die verbreitete Meinung entkräften, Benni Kamba 009 sei ein afrikanischer James Bond. Sicherlich hat er Ähnlichkeiten mit dem britischen Geheimagenten, und Maillu hat die Ziffer 009 nicht ohne Grund gewählt. Dennoch ist Benni Kamba ein Agent mit eigenen Charakterzügen und die Gleichsetzung mit den Romanen von Ian Fleming ist vermutlich nur durch die große Popularität der James Bond Filme entstanden.

1.2   David Maillu

David Gian Maillu ist wahrscheinlich der meist publizierte Autor Afrikas (Asego 2006). Er hat über 70 Bücher geschrieben, darunter Kinderbücher, Erzählungen, Prosa, Theaterstücke und Liedtexte. Er übersetzte englische Kinderbücher ins Kikamba, einer östlich von Nairobi gesprochenen Bantu-Sprache, und später auch Kikamba-Literatur ins Englische.

Beim Radio-Sender "Voice of Kenya" las er seine eigenen Gedichte. In der *Kenya Times* ist er mit einer eigenen Kolumne vertreten.

---

[1] "Literary critics have not been very generous in their assessment of Maillu's work. No one has lavished praise on him, and few have admitted finding any redeeming value in what or how he writes. The general feeling among serious academics appears to be that such literature is beneath criticism for it is wholly frivolous, the assumption being that a scholar should not waste his time on art that aims to be truly popular" (Lindfors 1991: 98).

1992 erhielt er den "Kenyatta Prize for Literature" und 1998 wurde ihm der Ehrendoktor-Titel für "African Literature and Political Philosophy" von der St Clements University Süd-Australien verliehen.

Geboren wurde Maillu 1939 in Machakos, östlich von Nairobi. Schon in früher Kindheit war es Maillus Lieblingsbeschäftigung Geschichten zu erzählen und sobald er schreiben lernte, begann er diese aufzuschreiben (Lindfors 1979a).

Aufgrund der Schwierigkeit als afrikanischer Schriftsteller Beachtung zu finden und publiziert zu werden, gründete Maillu Anfang der 70er Jahre seinen eigenen Verlag *Comb Books*, von dem er seine ersten Erfolge *Unfit for Human Consumption* (1973), *My Dear Bottle* (1973), *Troubles* (1974) und *After 4:30* (1974) drucken lies. Seine Themen waren gesellschaftliche Probleme oder Tabus, wie Alkohol und Sexualität, wobei seine direkte Art zu schreiben starke Kritik erfuhr. Niemand hatte zuvor die körperlichen und geistigen Dimensionen von Erotik und Alkoholismus in einer solchen Detailliertheit dargestellt.

> Yet in East Africa no one before Maillu had written about such matters in quite the same way, with so much attention focused on the physiological and psychological dimensions of erotic and dipsomaniac behavior. It was no doubt this unusual "frankness," as Maillu terms it, that won him so many readers. He talked dirty in a new way (Lindfors 1991: 90).

Trotz der starken Kritik an seinem Schreibstil, die im Jahr 1976 zu einem Verkaufsverbot seiner Bücher in Tansania und dem Schließen seines Verlags führten, waren seine Geschichten sehr beliebt, und die Bücher hatten verhältnismäßig hohe Auflagen. *Unfit For Human Consumption* wurde allein bis 1979 drei mal neu aufgelegt und *Troubles* wurde mit einer Stückzahl von 50.000 gedruckt (Lindfors 1979a).

Nachdem Maillu 1979 seinen neuen Verlag *David Maillu Publishers Ltd.* gründete, mit dem er als erstes sein Werk *Kadosa* (1979) veröffentlichte, änderte er seinen Schreibstil. Er schrieb weniger offensiv, legte mehr Wert auf Zwischenmenschlichkeit in der Darstellung seiner Charaktere. Trotzdem setzte er sich weiterhin mit gesellschaftlichen und politischen Problemen in seinen Werken auseinander.

Seine Bücher werden jedoch nicht wegen der sexuellen Erlebnisse ihrer Charaktere gelesen. Manche junge Autoren führten Maillus Erfolg nur auf die sexuellen Seiten seiner Bücher zurück. Sie versuchten seinen Stil zu kopieren und hatten mit ihrer, an Pornographie grenzenden, Literatur wenig Erfolg. Ein Fragebogen seines eigenen Verlages hat ergeben, dass viele Leser seine Bücher aus anderen Gründen lesen[2].

> You'd be astonished if you went through some of these questionnaires. People hardly talk about the
> sexy parts of my writing. But many other writers thought, "Well, if we write like this, we are going to
> get results." But some of them have been complete failures. I have found, and I believe, that Africans
> are not interested in reading just sexy things. To them, sex is just one of the many things that make a
> human being. Writers who overdo the sex theme thus make a serious blunder (Lindfors 1979a: 88).

In seinen zwei Romanen *Benni Kamba 009 in The Equatorial Assignment* (Macmillan Pacesetters, 1980) und *in Operation DXT* (Heinemann, 1986) ist der Erfolg der Bücher kaum auf die sexuellen Anspielungen zurückzuführen. Vielmehr ist es die Identifizierung mit dem Protagonisten Benni Kamba, der die afrikanische Welt mit Durchhaltevermögen und westlichem James Bond-Charme rettet, die zu der großen Leserschaft geführt hat.

2. Benni Kamba 009

2.1 Der Held

Benni Kamba 009 ist ein Aktion-Held, nach der Vorlage von Ian Flemings: *James Bond 007,* und stilistisch eine Adaption der James Hadley Chase-Thriller (Lindfors 1991: 93). Colonel Benni Kamba 009 ist Geheimagent und operiert für den afrikanischen Geheimdienst *National Intergrity Service of Africa, kurz* NISA, dessen geheime Basis in der Sahara stationiert ist. NISA bekämpft Kräfte, die den afrikanischen Kontinent und seine Bewohner bedrohen und auszubeuten versuchen.

Die Person Benni Kamba ist der des britischen Geheimagenten 007 in vielen Dingen sehr ähnlich: Er hat die Lizens zum Töten, er zieht Frauen magisch an, und seine „Kambagirls", die manchmal auch für den Gegenspieler arbeiten, verstehen es, ihn um den Finger zu wickeln. Benni Kamba fährt gern schnelle Autos, und begibt sich, manchmal auch ungewollt, in aussichtslose Situationen, und ist meistens an Ort und Stelle, wenn Hilfe gebraucht wird. Allerdings besitzt er auch Charakterzüge, die sein britischer Kollege nicht besitzt. Er ist nicht

---

[2] „People say that I hit the nail on the head, whatever that means. People say that they see themselves when they are reading the books; they can identify with situations and characters". (Lindfors 1979a: 87)

der coole, knallharte Geheimagent, wie James Bond ihn verkörpert; Benni Kamba hat in auswegslosen Situationen auch mal Angst um sein eigenes Leben. Außerdem kommt es bei ihm nicht mit jeder Frau die er trifft zum Geschlechtsakt (siehe 4.).

2.2 Die Handlung

2.2.1 Benni Kamba 009 in The Equatorial Assignment

The Equatorial Assignment ist der erste Auftrag von Benni Kamba 009 im Dienste von NISA. Er soll die Chengolama-Basis zerstören, deren Oberhaupt Dr. Thunder in allen afrikanischen Staaten Marionetten-Präsidenten einschleusen will, um die Staaten zu kontrollieren und auszubeuten. Dabei kommt ihm Colonel Swipta in die Quere, eine attraktive, dominante Frau, die ihn verführt und anschließend versucht durch eine Autobombe zu töten, was ihr jedoch misslingt. Benni Kamba erreicht die geheime Chengolama-Basis und findet Hilfe in der einheimischen Bevölkerung, die von dem neuen Chengolama-Präsidenten tyrannisiert wird. Sein Plan wird jedoch von Colonel Swipta vereitelt und er wird auf der Basis gefangen gehalten, wo er Dr. Thunder kennen lernt, und dessen zerstörerische Waffe ‚Thundercrust', ein Sprengsatz der sich erst tief in die Erde gräbt, bevor er detoniert. Mit dieser Waffe möchte Dr. Thunder die NISA-Basis zerstören, um seinen größten Widersacher zu vernichten.

Doch durch eine geschickte Taktik gelingt es Benni Kamba Colonel Swipta glauben zu machen, dass er sie liebt, und erschießt sie in ihrer Wohnung. Danach vernichtet er Dr. Thunder und lässt dessen Rakete auf der Chengolama-Basis detonieren.

2.2.2 Benni Kamba 009 in Operation DXT

Benni Kamba macht gerade Urlaub mit seiner neuen Liebe, Kristina, deren Leben er vor seinem ersten Auftrag in The Equatorial Assignment bei einem Autounfall gerettet hat. Während dessen wütet in Darba eine tödliche Krankheit, die durch die Droge DXT (Dhexaeto) ausgelöst wurde, ein allgemeines Mittel gegen Kopfschmerzen, Müdigkeit, Erkältung, das bei einer fünftägigen Anwendung ein Jahr gegen die Beschwerden vorbeugen soll. Es stellt sich jedoch heraus, dass die Patienten, die das Produkt eingenommen haben nach etwa zwanzig bis neunundzwanzig Monaten, einer Krankheit erliegen, die umgangssprachlich „Disconnector" genannt wird. Die Muskeln entlang des Rückenmarks verkrampfen sich, was zu einer Durchtrennung des Rückenmarks, und damit zum Tod führt. Zusätzlich wird die Region von starken Magenproblemen, Herzflimmern und Zahnausfall heimgesucht. Recherchen haben ergeben, das ein bestimmter importierter Zucker, für die Beschwerden verantwortlich ist, und gleichzeitig ein populäres Medikament gegen Magenbeschwerden und Herzflimmern in Umlauf ist, das den Zahnausfall auslöst. Auffäligerweise wird der Zucker und das Medikament von der gleichen Firma hergestellt. Eben dieser Hersteller, *Merritum and Co Limited* soll auch das Medikament DXT in Umlauf gebracht haben. Und ein weiteres Schiff mit der gefährlichen Ladung ist unterwegs nach Afrika.

Benni Kamba fliegt nach London, um die Machenschaften des Vorsitzenden von *Merritum and Co. Ltd.,* Mr O'Tloot aufzudecken. Begleitet wird er von Jos Miksi dem Minister für Außenhandel. Nachdem sie die junge, attraktive Tochter Miss O'Tloot kennen lernen, fliegen sie mit Mr und Miss O'Tloot nach Merritum Island, dem Hauptsitz von Merritum and Co Ltd. Nachdem der erste Versuch Benni Kambas die Fabriken zu zerstören und O'Tloot zu töten misslingt, und er gefangen genommen und gefoltert wird, schafft er es, sich zu befreien und seinen Auftrag zu erfüllen. Dabei verschont er Viora, die hübsche Adoptiv-Tochter von O'Tloot, und flüchtet mit ihr von der Insel. Ein Bodyguard überlebt jedoch, entführt Viora und es kommt zu einem letzten Gefecht auf dem Frachter bevor dieser mit seiner gefährliche Ladung vernichtet wird.

3. Der neue David Maillu

„The New David Maillu" ist ein Aufsatz von Bernth Lindfors (1991) betitelt, der das literarische Werk Maillus beleuchtet. Eine der Ansichten Lindfors ist, dass sich der Schreibstil Maillus dahingehend verändert hat, dass er weniger offensiv, weniger schmutzig und mit mehr Zurückhaltung schreibt:

> If we compare Maillu's latest works with those he wrote and published during Comb Books' brief heyday, one change becomes apparent immediately: the dirty talk is gone. His heroes may be sexually active but they are not sexually obsessed, and their physical interactions with members of the opposite sex tend to be described with restraint, even reticence" (Lindfors 1991: 90)

Diese Aussage lässt die Vermutung zu, das die Darstellung von Sexualität in Maillus Werk einen großen Stellenwert zur Bewertung dessen Popularität einnimmt.

Es ist zwar in der Tat so, das in den neueren Werken von David Maillu weniger die Sexualität im Vordergrund steht. Die Akteure haben zwar Verkehr mit Frauen, die Sexualität wird jedoch dem Leser nicht dargestellt, sondern nur angedeutet. Kann man aber aus diesem Grunde von einem neuen David Maillu sprechen? Hat sich denn Maillus Schreibstil verändert? Ich werde im folgenden aufzeigen, dass die Veränderungen in Maillus Werk und überhaupt der Erfolg seiner Bücher nicht auf die sexuellen Aspekte zurückzuführen sind.

Auf die Frage hin, warum seine Bücher ein so großes Publikum erreicht haben, antwortet Maillu:

> People say that I hit the nail on the head, whatever that means. People say that they see themselves when they are reading the books; they can identify with situations and characters. Basically, I think there are three things that tend to make the books popular. Humor is one, frankness may be another, and some people say the books contain wisdom, but I don't know what kind of wisdom that is (Lindfors 1979a: 87).

David Maillu ist in der Tat ein offensiver Schreiber, er spricht über die Probleme, über die man in Afrika meist ungern spricht. Sexualität, Trinksucht, gesellschaftliche Desorientierung und Korruption. Unter seinem ersten Verlagshaus Comb Books erscheinen Bücher, deren Protagonisten, in der Regel Männer aus dem öffentlichen Dienst in Nairobi, Sex mit vielen unterschiedlichen Frauen haben, und dabei oft nebenbei der Trinksucht erliegen. Auf Grund der Thematisierung von Sexualität wurden seine Bücher als pornographisch beschimpft, und sein Verlagshaus ging u.a. aufgrund des Verkaufsverbots in Tansania pleite, obwohl er mit seinem Schreibstil eine große Leserschaft in seinen Bann zog.

Die Unterstellung, das seine Bücher nur aufgrund der offenen Darstellung der Sexualität zu den, für afrikanische Verhältnisse, enormen Verkaufszahlen führten, ist nicht tragkräftig. Bei einem so produktiven Autor kann nicht nur die Thematik der Romane für deren Popularität ausschlaggebend sein, die sich ohnehin nicht nur auf Sex beschränkt, sondern Probleme aller Art des Großstadtlebens und des gesellschaftlichen Miteinander anspricht. Auch der Schreibstil scheint die Menschen zu bewegen. Sie können sich mit den Figuren identifizieren und deren Handlungsweisen nachvollziehen. Aus diesem Grund schreibt Maillu auch kaum über die Schönheiten des Lebens und macht keinen Hehl daraus, die Probleme anzusprechen, die Ostafrikaner bewegen.

> It has not been my interest to dwell on the beautiful or to set my stories in the nicer Part of the town. I want to point on some of the issues that people have to deal with in live. (…) because can make a contribution to society, you must say something about what is happening in the world, what is happening to people in East Africa (Lindfors: 1979a: 87).

Wenn man die Liste der Publikationen Maillus betrachtet, fällt einem auf, das sich keineswegs nur Werke mit detailgetreuer Darstellung des geschlechtlichen Aktes darunter befinden. Maillu ist ein Autor mit vielen Fassetten. Er variiert nicht nur in der Wahl der literarischen Form, die Kurzgeschichten, Poesie, Theaterstücke und Liedtexte, sowie zweisprachige Literatur umfasst (*Without Kiinua Mgongo*, Maillu Publishing House: 1989; Swahili – Englisch).

Auch die Thematik seiner Bücher ist mit Kindergeschichten, religiösen, politischen, philosophischen, sowie gesellschaftskritischen Texten und Unterhaltungsliteratur sehr umfangreich.

> "Maillu the moralist, Maillu the practical psychologist, Maillu the homespun philosopher, Maillu the comedian, Maillu the popular publisher, tries to provide the kind of stimulating entertainment that will the satisfy the mental hunger of his people and thereby help to sustain the "human life" in Kenya" (Lindfors 1991: 97).

David Maillu möchte mit seinen Büchern seine Leser unterhalten, und manchmal auch zur Einsicht ihrer Fehler bringen[3].

> "I rather like to believe I am an educator as well as an entertainer and that my books have a moral purpose. Perhaps this is why so many people read them" (Lindfors 1979a: 87).

Er probiert neue Formen aus, experimentiert sowohl mit seiner Kreativität, als auch mit den stilistischen Möglichkeiten der Literatur, und hat so die Grenzen seines Schaffens sowie der Literatur im allgemeinen weiter ausgedehnt als jeder andere Schriftsteller Afrikas.

> "Perhaps the most encouraging sign of Maillu's growth as a creative artist has been his willingness to

---

[3] „If an alcoholic reads My Dear Bottle and decides not to go out for drinks that night, it gives me satisfaction in the sense that I know I have helped him by occupying his mind with something else". (Lindfors 1979a: 87)

experiment with new forms and new ideas. [...]

Yet Maillu cannot be ignored in any systematic effort to understand the evolution of an East African literature, for he has extended the frontiers of that literature farther than any other single writer" (Lindfors 1991: 98).

Daher ist der ausschlaggebende Punkt, der zu der Popularität Maillus geführt hat nicht auf das Kriterium der sexuellen Darstellung zurück zuführen, sondern darauf, *was* und vor allem *wie* er schreibt.

Dass er in seinen Büchern der 1970er Jahre provozierender und offensiver schreibt, und sich in den neueren Werken in dieser Hinsicht zurückhält, ist wohl auch auf den Zeitgeist, aber vor allem auf das Alter Maillus zurückzuführen. Ein Autor wird keine Freude an seinem Schaffen finden, wenn er immer nur die gleiche Thematik und den gleichen Stil verwendet. Er ist darauf bedacht, sich zu entwickeln, neue Techniken auszuprobieren, seine Kreativität auszuschöpfen. Als junger Autor hatte Maillu gewiss eine andere Einstellung zur Gesellschaft und zur Literatur als heute. Seine Lebens- und Gesellschaftseinstellung hat sich im Laufe der Zeit entwickelt, und demenstprechend hat sich auch sein Schreibstil verändert.

Abgesehen davon wurden längst nicht alle Werke von David Maillu veröffentlicht. Solch eine Aussage ist natürlich nicht beweiskräftig und lässt sich nicht belegen. Was Maillu wirklich zu neuen Gedanken gebracht hat, lässt sich nur in einem Gespräch mit dem Autor herausfinden.

4.   Benni Kamba 009 als afrikanischer Agent –
Kopie oder Innovation?

Die beiden Romane *Benni Kamba 009 in the Equatorial Assignment* und *Benni Kamba 009 in Operation DXT* sind Musterbeispiele für die Experimentierfreude und die Kreativität Maillus. Benni Kamba 009 ist meines Wissens nach der einzige Agenten-Roman eines afrikanischen Schriftstellers, und der einzige, der augenscheinlich nach dem James Bond-Muster ,gestrickt' ist[4]. Doch dies ist nur vordergründig der Fall. Auf den ersten Blick fällt die

---

[4] Lindfors (1979b: 114) erwähnt einen „James Bond-type thriller" von Hilary Ng'weno ,The Men from Pretoria'.

Doppel-Null ins Auge, was einen direkten Vergleich mit James Bond 007 nahe legt.

Die Benni Kamba Romane sind in erster Linie reine Unterhaltungsstücke, wobei es immer wieder Anspielungen auf gesellschaftliche, afrikanische Missstände gibt. Themen dieser Art sind Armut, Polygamie und natürlich ‚white supremacy'. Der letzt genannte Punkt spiegelt sich vor allem in den Antagonisten der Figur Benni Kambas wider, die entweder versuchen, den afrikanischen Kontinent mit schädlichen Medikamenten und Industrie-Monopolen auszubeuten, oder durch Marionetten-Präsidenten die Herrschaft in Afrika an sich zu reißen. Wobei der Gegenspieler in *The Equatorial Assignment* kein Weißer, sondern ein Schwarzer ist, aber dennoch durch seine ‚weißen' Charakterzüge als Beispiel für ‚white supremacy' herangezogen werden kann.

In Benni Kamba 009 sind kaum sexuelle Darstellungen vorhanden. Der Protagonist interessiert sich zwar für diverse Frauen, und hat auch Affären mit der einen oder anderen, aber es kommt in keinem Fall zur literarisch-expliziten Ausführung des Geschlechtsaktes. Maillu beschreibt die geschlechtlichen Annäherungen eher spielerisch denn pornographisch (Lindfors 1991: 94).

> „The spent the night together in Kamba's flat. Very early in the morning, they swam far out to sea together. Obviously this girl was a powerful swimmer, too.
>
> 'I expected you last night.' Kamba shook the water from his head. They swam closely.
>
> 'You know what?' she said. 'I'm swimming naked, come and feel me.'
>
> He passed his hand over her breasts, then down there.
>
> 'Beware of the small fish!'(...)
>
> Their bodies slipped over each other. He kissed her and they sank into the water together and swam under it for a long distance, playing" (Maillu 1980: 35).

Maillu deutet zwar das Geschlechtsspiel der beiden Charaktere an, geht aber nicht mehr so weit, wie in manch anderen seiner Bücher, den eigentlichen Akt in allen Einzelheiten zu beschreiben. Auch in anderen Passagen ist diese Tendenz spürbar, im zweiten Benni Kamba, der sechs Jahre später erschienen ist, noch viel mehr. Hier wird geschickt, wie ein Schnitt in einem Filmstreifen, der entsprechende sexuelle Teil heraus geschnitten.

„The sand felt nice and cool under his feet. Her beach dress fluttered gaily in the breeze now and again showing some parts of her that should, by someone with perfect tact, not be seen. To Kamba it seemed that he was destined to fall into the hands of mysterious powerful women.

'Viora,' Benni Kamba called her name.

'Mmh?' she grinned into the wind.

'You are beautiful.'

She stopped walking instantly and stared at him. Fear cut through him that he might upset her. A thousand things ran through his mind.

[…]

He worried about what was going to come from her next. But all the same it felt good to be holding the hand of a wealthy girl. He felt something else, but he couldn't yet describe what it was. He liked her perfume and her voice.

[…]

When Viora and Kamba returned from the walk, she invited him to her father's mansion. This invitation, Benni Kamba appreciated, was the second landmark of his mission. As she took him round   the rooms, he waited with fear in case she peeled herself down to the skin and asked him to kiss her, or even made a more expensive request.

'If she asks me to kiss her,' Kamba asked himself, 'would I...?'

'What?' Benni interrupted. 'Why would you not do it? You know what, old chap? A kiss is an
opening to a larger home!'

[…]

'Mmh!' Benni Kamba said appreciatively. When Viora looked at him, he saw the reflection of the blue sea in her eyes. As they both stood silently on the verandah, it looked somehow as if each of them was playing a game of hide and seek with the other. (…)

'But,' Benni Kamba worried, 'I wonder whether, of all the men Viora has met, she was waiting to fall in love with a black man? Whatever happens,' he told himself while standing there, 'I should not touch her.'

[…]

They had a drink together, silently, still trying to hide their thoughts from each other. Benni Kamba felt that she was waiting for something from him, something that didn't come. Finaly she drove him back to his house before the storm started." (Maillu 1986: 91-92, 101-103)

In diesen etwas längeren Ausschnitten, wird vielleicht deutlich, wie Maillu die sexuelle Darstellung umgeht, und nur durch die Gedanken des Protagonisten dessen sexuellen Phantasien und Wünsche beschreibt.

Besonders interessant ist die Art und Weise, wie Maillu den britischen Agenten-Roman bzw. Agenten-Helden in einem afrikanischen Kontext umsetzt. Es ist nicht ausreichend, nur die Landschaft, das Klima und die Hautfarbe zu verändern. Wenn der Roman unter afrikanischen Lesern erfolgreich und beliebt sein soll, müssen die Wünsche und Bedürfnisse der Figuren den afrikanischen Hintergrund widerspiegeln, damit die Leser sich mit ihnen identifizieren können. Gleichzeitig muss die Geschichte aber auch einen Charme des Unbekannten und des Abenteuers ausstrahlen. Maillu gelingt es diese beiden Pole miteinander zu verbinden. Im folgenden sollen einige Beispiele angebracht werden, wie Maillu diese Schwierigkeit kreativ umsetzt.

Der britische Geheimdienst hat seinen Hauptsitz in London, Maillu distanziert sich von der Idee der Großstadt, da in afrikanischen Großstädten ein so enormes Bauvorhaben nicht leicht umzusetzen wäre, und auch nicht geheim gehalten werden könnte. Er entscheidet sich lieber für die menschenfeindliche Sahara, als über- und unterirdisches Geheimquartier.

James Bond fährt gerne schnelle und teure Autos. Benni Kamba fährt auch gerne schnell, doch da für die afrikanischen Straßenverhältnisse ein Sportwagen eher unvorteilhaft wäre, fährt er einen Citroën.

Maillu nutzt die korrupte politische Situation in einigen afrikanischen Staaten, und lässt einen afrikanischen Milliardär Marionetten-Präsidentschaften errichten, um die Herrschaft über den afrikanischen Kontinent zu gewinnen; nicht die Weltherrschaft.

Auch die Gesundheitssituation und die Angst vor tödlichen Krankheiten baut Maillu als Geschichtsgrundlage in seinen zweiten Benni Kamba 009 mit ein, sowie die Überproduktion und unwissende, nicht-sachgerechte Anwendung von Medikamenten.

Maillu verwendet bewusst eine andere Kennungs-Ziffer für den afrikanischen Agenten und betont den Symbolgehalt, der sich dahinter verbirgt:

Nach den Aussagen von Dr. Tripplo, der Chef des afrikanischen Geheimdienstes, haben die meisten Militärputsche im neunten Jahr der Unabhängigkeit ihrer Staaten stattgefunden, oder im 18., 27., 36., usw. Die 9 ist weiterhin ein Symbol für den Planeten Mars, für Eisen, für

Unbesiegbarkeit, für Ambition, Energie, Führungskraft und Dominanz. Außerdem hat die Ziffer 9 die Eigenschaft, dass sie, wenn multipliziert mit einer anderen Ziffer immer ein Produkt ergibt, dessen Ziffern, wenn sie miteinander addiert werden, wiederum 9 ergibt. Auch ist sie die letzte Ziffer in der Nummerierung. Die Neun ist die Nummer des schwarzen Mannes und Afrikas, und bedeutet dessen letztendliche Überlegenheit:

> „'[...]First we chose this number for its special qualities and symbolism; second, because it is the number of the black man, Africa. the African might comes late, just as the number 9 comes later after all the other numerical numbers, yet it is final and represents dominion. We know where we are going'" (Maillu, 1980: 54, f.).

Dieser Textausschnitt verdeutlicht sehr schön, dass es Maillu nicht nur um eine Adaption der James Bond Romane geht, sondern dass er mehr als nur Unterhaltungsliteratur schreiben wollte, die sich zumindest teilweise kritisch mit der sozialen und politischen Situation Afrikas auseinandersetzt.

Der größte Unterschied zwischen Bond 007 und Kamba 009 ist Benni Kambas Art mit Frauen umzugehen. Bond hat keine Gefühle für andere Frauen und wenn, dann nur oberflächlich. Kamba ist zwar mindestens genauso charmant wie James Bond, doch hat er nicht vor mit jeder Frau Sex zu haben. Für Kristina, die er im ersten Buch kennen lernt und im zweiten die Beziehung mit ihr vertieft, empfindet er sogar starke Gefühle, und hat vor sie eventuell zu heiraten. Maillu deutet auf diese innige Beziehung mit einer Geschichte in der Geschichte hin, ‚the story of absolute happiness'. Ein religiöser Mann fragt sich, ob man im Jenseits die gleichen Befriedigung, wie Heiraten, Essen, Spielen oder Sex haben könne, wie im Diesseits. Daraufhin bittet er Gott, er möge ihm zeigen, was wahres Glück sei. Gott sendet ihm einen überaus hübschen, mysteriösen Vogel, der für den Mann singt, aber immer wieder zum nächsten Baum fliegt. Der Mann ist ganz hingerissen, und folgt dem Vogel sieben Tage und sieben Nächte, und empfindet weder Hunger noch Durst. Bis der Vogel eines Tages verschwunden ist, und der Mann verwirrt, ohne zu wissen wo er ist, aus seiner Trance aufwacht:

> „'[...] But, curiously, he seemed to think that only a minute ago, he had been sitting outside his house basking in the sun. But what had happened? Where was he? He was shocked. More schocks came later to him when he learnt that he had been away for seven days following that mysterious bird, without ever sensing the passing of time or feeling hunger or worry, sensing absolutely nothing. During those seven days, he had experienced a piece of absolute happiness wrapped up in timelessness. While he lay

there, he heard a voice tell him, "John, rise and go home. That was the answer to your prayer. You have tasted a tiny bit of the eternal happiness"'

Kristina sighed and turned to face Benni Kamba. But Kamba was motionless and silent, staring with a faraway look at the ceiling, as if he, too, had discovered the bright blue-green happiness bird and now was watching it, mesmerised" (Maillu 1986: 50).

Hier wird deutlich, dass Benni Kamba eben doch kein James Bond ist. Er ist gefühlvoll, sensibel, nimmt sich Zeit für Kristina.

5.   Zusammenfassung

Ich habe versucht aufzuzeigen, das David Maillu im Gegensatz zur weitläufigen Meinung kein pornographischer Autor ist, und seine Popularität sich nicht nur anhand der sexuellen Aspekte seiner Bücher erklären lässt.

David Maillu ist ein höchst produktiver, kreativer und versierter Schriftsteller, dem man nicht nachsagen kann, das seine Werke nur von sexuellen, oder gar pornographischen Themen geprägt sind. Obwohl er sich in den Anfängen seiner Kariere viel mit dem Thema Sexualität auseinander gesetzt hat, schreibt er abwechslungsreich und experimentiert mit verschiedenen Stilen und Thematiken. Er schreibt über das, was ihn beschäftigt, und was die Leser interessiert und nicht was von einem kenianischen Autor erwartet wird. Mit recht schreibt Lindfors, er habe die Grenzen der Literatur weiter ausgedehnt als jeder andere Schriftsteller.

Desweiteren konnte ich aufzeigen, dass Maillu bemüht ist, nicht einfach das James Bond-Muster zu kopieren, sondern einen neue Romanfigur geschaffen hat, die adäquat dem afrikanischen Kontext angepasst ist, und ihre eigenen Charakterstärken besitzt. Ähnlichkeiten mit James Bond sind vorhanden, am nur vordergründig. Maillu wollte eben keinen schwarzen James Bond erschaffen, sondern einen afrikanischen Agenten-Helden, der als Zeichen für den afrikanischen Fortschritt und Loskettung von der weißen Unterdrückung steht.

Hat sich Maillus Schreibstil verändert? Ja. Der neue David Maillu schreibt aber mit Sicherheit nicht anders oder über andere Themen, weil seine Bücher in den siebziger Jahren verboten waren, sondern weil er, wie jeder andere Autor, an Erfahrungen dazu gewonnen hat und es mehr Dinge zu erzählen gibt, als nur erotische.

6. Literatur

Asego, Nicholas. 2006. *David Maillu: The man who treads where angels dread.* Cover
    Story in Moments - Entertainments, Arts & Culture. Saturday June 17, 2006. http://
    www.eastandart.net/mags/moments/articles.php?articleid=1143954084   06.01.2007
    15:5 Uhr

Kurtz, J. Roger & Robert M. Kurtz. 2002. *Language and ideology in Postcolonial Kenyan
    Literature.* In: Readings in African Popular Fiction. International African
    Institute, Indiana University Press, Oxford, London, Bloomington. S. 124-128.

Lindfors, Bernth. 1979a. *Interview with David G. Maillu.* In: The African Book
    Publishing Record. Vol. 5, 2. April 1979. S. 85-88.

—. 1979b. *East African Popular Literature in English.* In: Journal of Popular Culture.
    Vol. 13, 1. S. 106-115.

    http://pao.chadwyck.co.uk/journals/displayItemFromId.do?
    QueryType=journals&ItemID=b181#listItem47

—. 1991. *The New David Maillu.* In: Popular Literatures in Africa. Hrsg.: Bernth
    Lindfors. Africa World Press, Trenton, N.J. S. 87-100.

Maillu, David G. 1980. *Benni Kamba 009 in The Equatorial Assignment.* Macmillan
    Pacesetters Series. Macmillan Education Limited, London Basingstoke.

—. David G. 1986. *Benni Kamba 009 in Operation DXT.* Spear Books, Heinemann
    Educational Books, Nairobi.